Wetlands

Environmental Issues, Global Perspectives

Wetlands

James Fargo Balliett

SHARPE REFERENCE
an imprint of M.E. Sharpe, Inc.

SHARPE REFERENCE

Sharpe Reference is an imprint of M.E. Sharpe, Inc.

M.E. Sharpe, Inc.
80 Business Park Drive
Armonk, NY 10504

© 2010 by M.E. Sharpe, Inc.

Library of Congress Cataloging-in-Publication Data

Balliett, James Fargo.
Wetlands: environmental issues, global perspectives / James Fargo Balliett.
    p. cm.
Includes bibliographical references and index.
ISBN 978-0-7656-8226-0 (hardcover: alk. paper)
1. Wetlands—Environmental aspects. 2. Wetland ecology. 3. Wetland conservation. I. Title.

QH87.3.B35 2010
333.91'816—dc22   2010012119

Figures on pages 6, 16, 32, and 104 by FoxBytes.

Printed and bound in the United States of America

The paper used in this publication meets the minimum requirements of
American National Standard for Information Sciences
Permanence of Paper for Printed Library Materials,
ANSI Z 39.48.1984.

(c) 10 9 8 7 6 5 4 3 2 1

Publisher: Myron E. Sharpe
Vice President and Director of New Product Development: Donna Sanzone
Vice President and Production Director: Carmen Chetti
Executive Development Editor: Jeff Hacker
Project Manager: Laura Brengelman
Program Coordinator: Cathleen Prisco
Assistant Editor: Alison Morretta
Text Design: Patrice Sheridan
Cover Design: Jesse Sanchez

Contents

Over the past 150 years, the planet Earth has undergone considerable environmental change, mainly as a result of the increasing number of people living on it. Unprecedented population growth has led to extensive development and natural resource consumption. A population that numbered 978 million people worldwide in 1800 reached 6.7 billion in 2009 and, according to the United Nations, may well exceed 8 billion by 2028.

This sixfold growth in population has brought about both positive and negative outcomes. Developments in medicine, various natural and social sciences, and advanced technology have resulted in widespread societal improvements. One measure of this success, average life expectancy, has climbed substantially. In the United States, life expectancy was 39.4 years in 1850; by 2009, it had grown to 77.9 years.

Another major change for global nations and cultures has been the accessibility and sharing of information. Though once isolated by oceans and geography, few communities remain untouched by technological innovation. The construction of jumbo jet planes, the development of advanced satellites and computers, and the power of the Internet have made travel and information readily available to an unprecedented number of people.

Technological advances have allowed residents of just about anywhere on the planet to share events and information almost instantly. For example, images of an expedition on the summit of Mount Everest or a scientific investigation in the middle of the Atlantic Ocean can be posted online via satellite and viewed by billions of citizens worldwide. In addition, cumulative and individual environmental impacts now can be assessed faster and more comprehensively than in years past.

During the same period, however, regulated and unregulated residential and business development that consumes natural resources has had profound impacts on the global environment. Such impacts are evident in the clear-cutting or burning of forests, whether this deforestation is for fuel or building materials, or simply to clear the land for other activities; the drainage of wetlands to divert freshwater, expand agriculture, or provide more building upland; the overfishing of oceans to meet an ever-growing appetite for seafood; the stripping of mountaintops for fuel, metals, or minerals; and the pollution of freshwater sources by the waste output of industrial and residential communities. In fact, pollution has spread across land, air, and water biomes in ever-increasing concentrations, causing considerable damage, especially to fragile ecosystems.

The Emergence of a Global Perspective

Environmental Issues, Global Perspectives provides a fresh look at critical environmental issues from an international viewpoint. The series consists of five individual volumes: *Wetlands, Forests, Mountains, Oceans,* and *Freshwater.* Relying on the latest accepted principles of science—the acquisition of knowledge based on reasoning, experience, and experiments—each volume presents information and analysis in a clear, objective manner. The overarching goal of the series is to explore how human population growth and behavior have changed the world's natural areas, especially in negative ways, and how modern society has responded to the challenges these changes present—often through increased educational efforts, better conservation, and management of the environment.

Each book is divided into three parts. The first part provides background information on the biome being discussed: how such ecosystems are formed, the relative size and locations of such areas, key animal and plant species that tend to live in such environments, and how the health of each biome affects our planet's environment as a whole. All five titles present the most recent scientific data on the topic and also examine how humans have relied on each biome for survival and stability, including food, water, fuel, and economic growth.

The second part of each book contains in-depth chapters examining seven different geographically diverse locations. An overview of each area details its unique features, including geology, weather conditions, and endemic species. The text also examines the health of the natural environment and discusses the local human population. Short- and long-term environmental impacts are assessed, and regional and international efforts to address interrelated social, economic, and environmental issues are presented in detail.

The third part of each book studies how the cumulative levels of pollution and aggressive resource consumption affect each biome on a global scale. It provides readers with examples of local and regional impacts—filled-in wetlands, decimated forests, overdeveloped mountainsides, empty fishing grounds, and polluted freshwater—as well as responses to these problems. Although each book's conclusion is different, scenarios are highlighted that present collective efforts to address environmental issues. Sometimes, these unique efforts have resulted in a balance between resource conservation and consumption.

The *Environmental Issues, Global Perspectives* series reveals that—despite the distance of geography in each title's case studies—a common set of human-induced ecological pressures and challenges turns up repeatedly. In some areas, evidence of improved resource management or reduced environmental impacts is positive, with local or national cooperation and the application of new technology providing measurable results. In other areas, however, weak laws or unenforced regulations have allowed environmental damage to continue unchecked: Brazen frontiersmen continue to log remote rain forests, massive fishing trawlers still use mile-long nets to fill their floating freezers in the open ocean, and communities, businesses, vehicles, factories, and power plants continue to pollute the air, land, and water resources. Such existing problems and emerging issues, such as global climate change, threaten not just specific animal and plant communities, but also the health and well-being of the very world we live in.

Wetlands

Wetlands encompass a diversity of habitats that rely on the presence of water to survive. Over the last two centuries, these hard-to-reach areas have been viewed with disdain or eliminated by a public that saw them only as dangerous and worthless lowlands. The *Wetlands* title in this series tracks changing perceptions of one of the world's richest and biologically productive biomes and efforts that have been undertaken to protect many areas. With upland and coastal development resulting in the loss of more than half of the world's wetlands, significant efforts now are under way to protect the 5 million square miles (13 million square kilometers) of wetlands that remain.

In *Wetlands*, three noteworthy examples demonstrate the resilience of wetland plants and animals and their ability to rebound from human-induced pressures: In Central Asia, the Aral Sea and its adjacent wetlands show promising regrowth, in part because of massive hydrology projects being implemented to undo years of damage to the area. The Everglades wetlands complex, spanning the lower third of Florida, is slowly reviving as restorative conservation measures are implemented. And Lake Poyang in southeastern China has experienced increased ecological health as a result of better resource management and community education programs focused on the vital role that wetlands play in a healthy environment.

Forests

Forests are considered the lungs of the planet, as they consume and store carbon dioxide and produce oxygen. These biomes, defined as ecological communities dominated by long-lived woody vegetation, historically have provided an economic foundation for growing nations, supplying food for both local and distant markets, wood for buildings, firewood for fuel, and land for expanding cities and farms. For centuries, industrial nations such as Great Britain, Italy, and the United States have relied on large tracts of forestland for economic prosperity.

The research presented in the *Forests* title of this series reveals that population pressures are causing considerable environmental distress in even the most remote forest areas. Case studies provide an assessment of illegal logging deep in South America's Amazon Rain Forest, a region closely tied to food and product demands thousands of miles away; an examination of the effect of increased hunting in Central Africa's Congo forest, which threatens wildlife, especially mammal species with slower reproductive cycles; and a profile of encroachment on old-growth tropical forests on the Southern Pacific island of Borneo, which today is better managed, thanks to the collective planning and conservation efforts of the governments of Brunei, Indonesia, and Malaysia.

Mountains

Always awe-inspiring, mountainous areas contain hundreds of millions of years of history, stretching back to the earliest continental landforms. Mountains are characterized by their distinctive geological, ecological, and biological conditions. Often, they are so large that they create their own weather patterns. They also store nearly one-third of the world's freshwater—in the form of ice and snow—on their slopes. Despite their daunting size and often formidable climates, mountains are affected by growing local populations, as well as by distant influences, such as air pollution and global climate change.

The case studies in the *Mountains* book consider how global warming in East Africa is harming Mount Kenya's regional population, which relies on mountain runoff to irrigate farms for subsistence crops; examine the fragile ecology of the South Island mountains in New Zealand's Southern Alps and consider how development threatens the region's endemic plant and animal species; and discuss the impact of mountain use over time in New Hampshire's White Mountains, where stricter management efforts have been used to limit the growing footprint of millions of annual visitors and alpine trekkers.

Oceans

Covering 71 percent of the planet, these saline bodies of water likely provided the unique conditions necessary for the building blocks of life to form billions of years ago. Today, our oceans continue to support life in important ways: by providing the largest global source of protein in the form of fish populations, by creating and influencing weather systems, and by absorbing waste streams, such as airborne carbon.

Oceans have an almost magnetic draw—almost half of the world's population lives within a few hours of an ocean. Although oceans are vast in size, exceeding 328 million cubic miles (1.37 billion cubic kilometers), they have been influenced by and have influenced humans in numerous ways.

The case studies in the *Oceans* title of this series focus on the most remote locations along the Mid-Atlantic Ridge, where new ocean floor is being formed 20,000 feet (6,100 meters) underwater; the Maldives, a string of islands in the Indian Ocean, where increasing sea levels may force residents to abandon some communities by 2020; and the North Sea at the edge of the Arctic Ocean, where fishing stocks have been dangerously depleted as a result of multiple nations' unrelenting removal of the smallest and largest species.

Freshwater

Freshwater is our planet's most precious resource, and it also is the least conserved. Freshwater makes up only 3 percent of the total water on the planet, and yet the majority (1.9 percent) is held in a frozen state in glaciers, icebergs, and polar ice fields. This leaves only 1.1 percent of the total volume of water on the planet as freshwater available in liquid form.

The final book in this series, *Freshwater,* tracks the complex history of the steady growth of humankind's water consumption, which today reaches some 3.57 quadrillion gallons (13.5 quadrillion liters) per year. Along with a larger population has come the need for more drinking water, larger farms requiring greater volumes of water for extensive irrigation, and more freshwater to support business and industry. At the same time, such developments have led to lowered water supplies and increased water pollution.

The case studies in *Freshwater* look at massive water systems such as that of New York City and the efforts required to transport this freshwater and protect these resources; examine how growth has affected freshwater quality in the ecologically unique and geographically isolated Lake Baikal region of eastern Russia; and study the success story of the privatized freshwater system in Chile and consider how that country's water sources are threatened by climate change.

Acknowledgments

I owe the greatest debt to my wonderful Mom and Dad, Nancy and Whitney, who led me to the natural world as a child. Thank you for encouraging curiosity and creativity, and for teaching me to be strong in the midst of a storm. I also could not have gotten this far without steady support, expert advice, and humorous optimism from my siblings: Blue, Julie, Will, and Whit.

I greatly appreciate the input of Dr. Arri Eisen, Director of the Program in Science and Society at Emory University, at key stages of this project. My sincere thanks also go to the superb team at M.E. Sharpe, including Donna Sanzone, Cathy Prisco, and Laura Brengelman, as well as Gina Misiroglu, Jennifer Acker, Deborah Ring, Patrice Sheridan, and Leslee Anderson. Any title that explores science and the environment faces daunting hurdles of ever-changing data and a need for the highest accuracy. This series benefited greatly from their precise work and steady guidance.

Finally, *Environmental Issues, Global Perspectives* would not have been possible without the efforts of the many scientists, researchers, policy experts, regulators, conservationists, and writers with a vested interest in the environment.

The last few decades of the twentieth century brought a significant change in awareness and attitudes toward the health of this planet. Scholars and laypeople alike shifted their view of the environment from something simply to be consumed and conquered now to a viewpoint of it as a significant asset because of its capacities for such measurable benefits as flood control, water filtration, oxygen creation, pollution storage and processing, and biodiversity support, as well as other positive features.

Knowledge of Earth's finiteness and vulnerability has resulted in substantially better stewardship. My thanks go to those people who, through their visions and hard work, have taught the next generation that fundamental science is essential and that humankind's collective health is inextricably tied to the global environment.

James Fargo Balliett
Cape Cod, Massachusetts

INTRODUCTION
TO WETLANDS

1 Understanding Wetlands

From a distance, a wetland appears as a harsh and dangerous place. Seemingly endless swarms of hungry mosquitoes and other flying insects, strong odors, shallow standing water, and deep mud often dominate the landscape. There are interwoven stands of trees, shrubs, and vines, often so dense that you cannot get through them without a struggle. There are poisonous snakes, carnivorous alligators and crocodiles, and not a lot of dry and solid ground on which to stand.

For centuries, these ecological areas have been the bane of nearby towns and cities as places that could not be built upon and where deadly disease and other dangers awaited those who dared to enter. Scientific research, however, has proven that wetlands are not any more threatening than a forest, a field, or a mountain. In fact, they are teeming with diverse forms of life, hosting thousands of thriving species. As understanding of these complex ecosystems and the abundant life that flourishes within them grows, the historic discomfort with wetlands has been evolving into a more accepting outlook. Indeed, knowledge that wetlands play a central role in the health and survival of Earth's species is more commonplace than in the past.

In sum, wetlands filter pollutants, offer protection against flooding by coastal storms, consume carbon dioxide and generate large volumes of oxygen, hold and slowly release storm water runoff, provide shelter and secluded habitat for wildlife, and support a biodiversity of birds, insects, amphibians, reptiles, and other animals in unique aquatic and terrestrial conditions. These and other valuable functions prove the overwhelming importance of wetlands to human and animal life across the planet. Based on such beneficial effects, wetlands also are known as "carbon

sinks," because they contain substantial vegetation growth and decaying matter that often is held in a preserved state in a low oxygen environment. This allows for the long-term storage of up to 30 percent of the global carbon.

What Are Wetlands?

Wetlands have been defined almost fifty times, in varying ways, by scientific organizations and government bodies. However, one definition, written in an international treaty in 1971 called the Ramsar Convention, stands out: areas of marsh, fen, peatland, or water, whether natural or artificial, permanent or temporary, with water that is static or flowing, fresh, brackish, or salt.

Water is the key to a wetland's existence, whether it is inundated by surface water or groundwater. Wetlands occur in both freshwater and salt water. Some wetlands, in coastal areas, have adapted to a mix of the two, called brackish water. In general, this ecosystem is a transitional habitat that occurs between upland (terrestrial) and open water (aquatic) environments.

Water carries the range of nutrients, organic matter, and minerals that living plants and organisms require. The water in a wetland also holds two very important gases, carbon dioxide and oxygen, in dissolved states. Plants consume both of these gases through their roots, and fish and amphibians breathe oxygen through their gills and skin. Overall, wetlands take in carbon dioxide and release oxygen.

The coffee-colored Loxahatchee River in southeastern Florida contains ten distinct freshwater and saltwater habitats. This 260-square-mile (673-square-kilometer) ecosystem provides homes for a wide variety of fish, birds, other wildlife, and plants, including dense stands of ferns and palms. *(Panoramic Images/Getty Images)*

Examples of wetlands include low-lying areas next to streams, ponds, coastal harbors, the adjacent areas and flood zones of a river, and even parts of a man-made drainage system. Such areas are present in every country around the world, from warm tropical areas to the frozen tundra.

Across the globe, wetlands make up about 6 percent of the planet's surface. The Millennium Ecosystem Assessment, performed by the Washington, D.C.–based World Resources Institute in 2005, estimates that there are approximately 4.9 million square miles (12.7 million square kilometers) of wetlands on Earth. This total area equates to an area 33 percent larger than the United States.

Approximately 2 percent of global wetlands are found in the form of lakes, 15 percent are floodplains, 20 percent are swamps, 26 percent are fens, and 30 percent are bogs.

Types of Wetlands

Wetlands are broken down into two basic groups: saltwater and freshwater. According to the U.S. Fish and Wildlife Service, saltwater wetlands include tidal marshes and mangrove swamps; freshwater wetlands include marshes (such as wet meadows, prairie potholes, vernal pools, and playa lakes), swamps (forested, shrub, and mangrove), and bogs (common, pocosin, and fen).

Coastal wetlands often form in an estuary, a semi-enclosed, primarily saltwater body with freshwater flowing into it from one or more sources. These are called estuarine wetlands, and the plant and animal species that live in these ecosystems commonly have unique adaptations to cope with the mix of freshwater and salt water. Coastal wetlands make up roughly 10 percent of global wetlands.

A tidal marsh often is found within a well-established estuary, and it contains a diversity of soft-stemmed vegetation that grows in the saturated water of the tides. Consisting of grasses and sedges, this kind of vegetation anchors itself in mud and sand flats and frequently forms the first line of defense against flooding and erosion caused by coastal storms. Tidal marshes are more common in temperate regions than in arctic or tropical climates.

Another type of coastal wetland, a saltwater mangrove swamp, thrives in more tropical regions. The vegetation that occupies this kind of wetland varies according to its exposure to salt water or freshwater, the type of soil in the swamp, and the depth of the water. There are nearly eighty different types of mangrove trees, including the distinctive red mangrove tree (*Rhizophora mangle*), which is known for its arching roots that climb up above the water's surface.

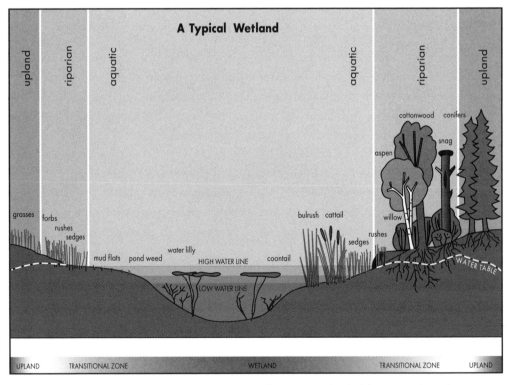

This figure shows a cross section and the basic contours of a typical wetland, delineating where plant species become established at certain locations relative to the presence of water. Plants also are affected by seasonal variations in the water level, which are indicated by the low and high water lines.

GLOBAL WETLANDS ESTIMATE, 2005

Country/Region	Square Miles	Square Kilometers
Africa	467,000	1.2 million
Asia	787,000	2 million
Europe	996,000	2.6 million
Neotropics	1.6 million	4.2 million
North America	934,000	2.4 million
Oceania	138,000	357,000
Estimated Total:	4.9 million	12.7 million

Source: Millennium Ecosystem Assessment, World Resources Institute, 2005.

Freshwater wetlands make up the remaining 90 percent of wetlands across the globe and appear adjacent to or within a wide range of water-supplying locations, including streams, rivers, ponds, lakes, and floodplains. Freshwater marshes, also called lacustrine wetlands (*lacus* means "lake" in Latin), often are found in small depressions near such waterways.

Freshwater Marshes

Freshwater marshes contain mineral-rich soils that consist of large amounts of organic materials and a mixture of clay, sand, and silt. These soils support wetland vegetation such as water lilies, reeds, bulrushes, and cattails. Water levels in these marshes may vary from a few inches to several feet deep.

There are a number of smaller marsh-like wetlands that occur in areas with poor drainage. These include wet meadows, which form in low-lying areas of farmland or hilly terrain. These meadows typically go through a wet season and then a drier season, when the surface water may disappear entirely.

Prairie potholes are freshwater meadows defined by small glacial depressions that fill with water after snowmelt or spring rains. Some are deeper than others (up to 1 foot, or about 0.3 meters), and these potholes often remain year-round, supporting established wetland vegetation and wildlife.

A vernal pool is typically a small wetland that fills with water during the winter and spring and contains little to no standing water during the rest of the year. These smaller wetlands usually are formed atop a clay lens (a concave layer) that holds water. They range from a few inches to a few feet in depth and generally are isolated within forested habitats. Vernal pools are frequented by amphibians such as the spotted salamander (*Ambystoma maculatum*).

A final type of freshwater marsh is a playa lake, a round shallow depression found in high plains environments. Some are carved out over time by wind. These flat-bottomed areas fill with water after rain or snow and dry out when there is less precipitation and in warmer months.

Freshwater Swamps

Several types of freshwater swamp wetlands exist in varying terrains, including forested areas, shrublands, and mangroves. They feature rich soils that support a variety of woody vegetation such as the red maple (*Acer rubrum*) in temperate climates or the tupelo tree (*Nyssa aquatica*) in subtropical areas.

A forested swamp contains dense trees 15 to 60 feet (5 to 18 meters) high. While it often is inundated with floodwaters from adjacent rivers or streams, this type of swamp rarely becomes completely dry. Forested swamps support vegetation that thrives when roots are underwater, including the pin oak tree (*Quercus palustris*) in colder areas and the bald cypress tree (*Taxodium distichum*) in warmer climates.

VISITING A WETLAND

To experience the richness of a wetland, visit one in your community. You likely can find a wetland near a river, stream, pond, or coastal waterway, and some wetlands are protected in public parks or preserves.

Visiting a wetland is not like climbing a mountain—the goal is not to trudge into the middle. Instead, approach your visit as if you are on a scientific expedition to discover the uniqueness of this place. If available, bring along a map of the area, as well as binoculars and a pen and notebook to record your observations.

Walk to the edge of the wetland and look around. Stand as quietly as you can. Listen for any activity—red-winged blackbirds singing, frogs calling, insects buzzing, small animals moving in the vegetation, or running water. Make notes of what you see, hear, and smell.

Move around the wetland, and repeat this inventory from several vantage points. You will recognize the biological diversity within the wetland's boundaries: a wide variety of insects, birds, animals, reptiles, amphibians, trees, shrubs, grasses, and other vegetation. Be patient. You will be amazed by what you discover.

A shrub swamp is similar to a forested swamp, but it is smaller in size and features less water and shallower soils. Often found along slow-moving streams and adjacent to wide floodplains, shrub swamps support vegetation that grows lower to the ground, such as the swamp rose (*Rosa palustris*), and feature fewer trees than a forested swamp.

Lastly, a freshwater mangrove swamp, similar to the aforementioned saltwater mangrove swamp, is commonly found in tropical and subtropical regions but is located farther inland from the coast. Such swamps feature the black mangrove (*Avicennia germinas*) and the white mangrove (*Laguncularia racemosa*), both of which have root projections called pneumatophores to help the tree obtain oxygen from water and soils.

Freshwater Bogs

Another freshwater wetland is a bog, known for a layer of spongy vegetation, called sphagnum or peat moss, that rests on top of open water. Commonly, bogs are established in old glacial depressions in colder climates and rely upon groundwater, rainfall, and snowmelt to thrive. The water is typically acidic and nearly stagnant. Vegetation and wildlife that inhabit these areas include the northern pitcher plant (*Sarracenia purpurea*) and the North American moose (*Alces alces*). The peat from larger bogs is often commercially harvested for use as a gardening mulch.

A pocosin bog, named after the Native American term meaning "swamp on a hill," is dominated by a mix of evergreens and shrubs. These areas often have little standing water but have saturated soil that reaches across large areas of flat upland. Soil in pocosins typically is poor in nutrients, and this limits the size and diversity of vegetation such wetlands can support.

The last type of bog is a fen, which differs from a typical bog, because it is not acidic but almost neutral in pH (a measure of acidity or alkalinity). A fen is supported by a groundwater source that enriches a diversity of vegetation, including rushes, sedges, grasses, and wildflowers. Found only in colder climates, a fen relies on a delicate chemical balance and easily can become a traditional bog if nutrients decline and mosses dominate the surface area.

Wetland Formation and Succession

There are four ways that wetlands are formed. These include plate tectonics (resulting in volcanic activity and earthquakes), land erosion, glacial activity, and human creation. Some processes happen in combination and others are isolated, but all allow water to be held in landforms.

The oldest way a wetland is formed is through plate tectonics. The planet Earth has an outer layer of bedrock that is broken into fifteen large and forty-one smaller tectonic plates, and they undergo a continual process of movement and collision with each other. Sometimes, a vein of lava emerges between plates to form volcanoes.

The impact of two or more plates colliding also causes the release of considerable energy in the form of earthquakes. Earthquakes can cause sudden, significant changes in the landscape. The Reelfoot Lake in northwestern Tennessee, now a national wildlife refuge, was formed in an earthquake in 1811, creating a 12-by-5-mile (19-by-8-kilometer) lake with adjacent wetlands.

The landmasses formed by the tectonic plates are then shaped over millions of years by land erosion due to gradual weathering and other natural forces. Exposure to wind, precipitation, and water movement gradually carves and reshapes these landmasses, creating new riverbeds, streambeds, and other depressions in sediment and bedrock.

Land erosion also occurs when ocean water impacts coastal land, forming wetland habitats. Each time a major tidal event, flood, or storm erodes part of the coastal landscape, a wetland may be established. These altered areas where water remains (often in a depression) may contain mineral-enriched soils that support vegetation and animal life.

A significant number of wetlands were formed by glacial activity. There have been several periods when extremely cold temperatures dominated the planet; these periods are referred to as ice ages. The most recent ice age occurred during the Pleistocene Epoch, beginning about 1.5 million years ago and ending roughly 14,000 years ago.

An example of the power of moving ice can be seen in the United States along the northeastern seaboard. Enormous sheets of ice, as thick as a mile in some places, covered up to 30 percent of the continent. One sheet in particular—called the Laurentide Ice Sheet—was formed 95,000 years ago. Around 23,000 years ago, it extended across coastal areas off Massachusetts; as its path fluctuated, it deposited large amounts of sand and rock. A resultant glacial moraine formed a 65-mile-long (105-kilometer-long) peninsula that became known as Cape Cod. This pockmarked landscape was ideal for both freshwater and saltwater wetlands. The Cape contains up to 1,000 freshwater kettle ponds, the result of large blocks of ice being left behind after the glaciers receded.

When the climate warmed, the glaciers retreated, and depressions were created wherever huge chunks of ice melted away. These icebergs sunk, melted, and formed kettle lakes with adjacent wetlands. The deposition of materials, including dense clay formed in a lens, also resulted in trapped water and the formation of vernal pool wetlands.

The last method of wetland formation is human activity. Early Mesopotamian farmers, living in what is today known as Iraq, beginning around 3000 B.C.E., engineered their fields for irrigation by impounding water during wet seasons and releasing it during dry seasons. This irrigation resulted in a number of new wetlands.

The study of artificial wetlands began in the middle of the twentieth century. Researchers noted that when polluted water ran into a dense section of submerged vegetation, much cleaner water was eventually released. Wetland scientists studied the efficiency of this system and designed "replicated" wetlands. Ranging in size from a quarter of an acre to hundreds of acres, these manufactured wetlands can serve as excellent sites to process storm water runoff, pollution from industrial activities, or treated human wastewater.

One example of wetlands being used to recover land damaged by industrial activities sits along the 219-mile-long (352-kilometer-long) Morava River in the Slovak Republic in Central Europe. Years of gravel mining adjacent to the river resulted in severe pollution from sediment-laden runoff; gravel pits filled with water and were abandoned. By planting numerous wetland species in the disturbed areas, many of the polluted landforms have been restored to healthy wetlands.

Evolving Ecosystems

Wetlands are not permanent habitats. Some may exist for only a few decades, while others last for centuries. Influences such as earthquakes, ocean surges, floods, or fire can eliminate a wetland within days.

If left in a natural state, wetlands undergo a series of changes over time, called succession. One example involves vegetation altering a wetland's size. A common freshwater plant called pondweed (from the family *Potamogetonaceae*) lives in many wetlands. As these plants grow and die, their decaying matter builds up and adds organic content and nutrients to the land underwater. When this has occurred for hundreds of years, the depression that the wetland previously occupied becomes filled in by new soil. Eventually, water levels reach only a few inches in depth, a forest emerges, and the wetland vanishes.

Another example of change is due to a variation in water levels, such as a reduction of water brought about by environmental shifts. Plant and animal species that relied on the previous water level and conditions die off or leave the area.

In both of these examples of succession, the result is a different form of wetland or none at all. A fen that is covered with sphagnum moss eventually will become an acidic bog due to vegetation growth. A coastal estuary that faces rising water levels from the ocean eventually will support only salt-loving

One of Ireland's most distinctive wetlands, bogs cover one-sixth of the island nation. Peat is farmed for industrial and domestic uses such as providing fuel for heating and enrichment of garden soil. *(Glen Allison/Photographer's Choice/Getty Images)*

species, as less and less freshwater mixes with the tides. These are all elements of succession, which is a normal part of the evolution of wetlands.

The Value of Wetlands

One important value of a wetland is floodwater protection. When major storms occur, rain and floodwater are held by a wetland through several actions. Water is trapped within the boundaries of the wetland, it is held in the soil, and it is absorbed by the plants. This water is then slowly released, filtered by the vegetation, sand, and sediments, running downstream or into a groundwater aquifer, where it recharges a water supply.

During Hurricane Ike's 2008 landfall into southern Louisiana, storm surges up to 20 feet (6 meters) high impacted the coast. Adjacent saltwater and freshwater wetlands played a pivotal role by absorbing up to 1.5 million gallons (5.7 million liters) of water. Salt marshes, anchored in sediment, and forested wetlands, such as mangrove swamps, provided shelter from the damaging force of the hurricane. By holding and then slowly releasing water, the hydrologic impact of the storm was greatly reduced.

Wetlands are able to provide several types of filtration for both water and air. Water that emerges from a wetland is much cleaner than when it arrived. In order to improve water quality, wetlands rely on a combination of plants that use organic and mineral contents, sand, and sediments to filter and trap pollutants and large amounts of microbiological bacteria and algae that consume a variety of chemicals. New research has shown that, working in concert, wetland plants and microbiological bacteria can tackle severe pollution.

When land and waterways were damaged in the town of Richmond, California, by oil refineries releasing selenium (a radioactive trace element) wetlands were created in 1999 to capture the runoff. Samples taken five years later revealed that up to 80 percent of the selenium had been consumed by biological processes and that the only by-product was a harmless gas.

Gaseous conversions are another key element of wetland functions. Plants and bacteria in a wetland work to convert carbon dioxide into oxygen, as well as to consume excess nitrogen and phosphorus. This extra oxygen then supports animal populations such as amphibians, which eat the vegetation, and fish, which, in turn, support bird and other animal populations.

A newly realized value of wetlands involves the carbon cycle. Too much carbon has been released into the atmosphere and is causing global warming. Although carbon is released through natural cycles, such as organic decay and volcanic eruption, human pollution discharged from automobiles, factories, and power plants has become a major contributor to increased carbon output. The global atmospheric carbon concentration in 1890 was 154 parts per million; in 2009, it was 387 parts per million.

Wetlands are able to sequester, or store, carbon inside living plants and in the soil and decaying organic matter surrounding the plants' roots. An illustration of this process can be found in peat bogs. These wetlands hold carbon in two ways, in the living peat and in the dead peat held in the soils. Global peat deposits have been estimated to contain up to 500 gigatons (1 gigaton is equal to 1 billion tons, or 2 trillion pounds) of carbon.

For centuries, wetlands also have offered substantial additional value to humans. Societies have used wetlands for a range of agricultural purposes, including farming and commercial fishing, and man-made wetlands treat septic and storm water runoff. Aesthetically, wetlands are beautiful, and popular recreational activities such as fishing, bird watching, camping, and hiking occur in or near them. Educationally, wetlands offer a power-packed classroom and laboratory, where students can observe and study everything from frogs to fungus to fireflies.

Therefore, estimating the monetary value of wetlands is a complex exercise, given the variability of types, conditions, and functions. If the goal is to protect or enhance a wetland, the market may value it differently than if the site is to be filled and a government building built upon it. In 2000, examples of replacement costs for destroyed wetlands ranged from $24,000 an acre for a mangrove swamp, to $49,000 an acre for a saltwater marsh, and $124,000 an acre for a forested freshwater wetland.

Selected Web Sites

Great Britain Wetlands Organization: http://www.wwt.org.uk.
Ramsar Convention on Wetlands: http://www.ramsar.org.
U.S. Environmental Protection Agency: http://www.epa.gov.
U.S Fish and Wildlife Service: http://www.fws.gov.
U.S. Geological Survey: http://www.usgs.gov.
Wetlands International: http://www.wetlands.org.

Further Reading

Batzer, Darold, ed. *Ecology of Freshwater and Estuarine Wetlands.* Berkeley: University of California Press, 2007.

Cronk, Julie. *Wetland Plants: Biology and Ecology.* Boca Raton, FL: CRC, 2001.

Dugan, Patrick. *Guide to Wetlands.* Buffalo, NY: Firefly, 2005.

Fraser, Lauchlan, and Paul A. Keddy, eds. *The World's Largest Wetlands: Ecology and Conservation.* Cambridge, UK: Cambridge University Press, 2005.

Mitsch, William, and James G. Gosselink. *Wetlands.* Hoboken, NJ: John Wiley and Sons, 2007.

World Resources Institute. *Millennium Ecosystem Assessment: Wetlands and Water.* Washington, DC: World Resources Institute, 2005.

2 Hydrology of Wetlands

Each wetland is varied in size and utilizes water in different ways. The movement and quality of water are measured through the science of hydrology, which comes from the Greek term *hydrologia,* meaning the "study of water." Hydrology plays a critical role in a wetland's health and biotic stability. A wetland depends on the inflow and outflow of water, called the hydrologic cycle, to maintain healthy levels of nutrients, sediment, and organic matter.

Wetlands get water from two main sources: precipitation and groundwater inflow. Precipitation may arrive in a wetland as rainfall, condensed water from fog, or snow. Such precipitation provides the wetland with water that can be stored in low-lying depressions and vegetation and, over time, can be slowly released. Sources of groundwater inflow include lakes, ponds, rivers, streams, and infiltration from underground springs or aquifers. A wetland's surface water can leave the area through stream outflow or through downward infiltration into the ground.

Wetlands host a number of additional hydrologic cycle events, including evaporation, condensation, and transpiration. As air temperatures increase, water turns from a solid—either in the form of snow or ice—to a liquid, then to a gas. Water turning from liquid to gaseous form is called evaporation. Up to 80 percent of all evaporation comes from saltwater seas and oceans, and 20 percent comes from freshwater sources.

As weather systems move in and out of a wetland, ambient air temperature changes result in water changing from a gas to a liquid and vice versa. If plants are cold and warm air rushes across them, water droplets will form on the

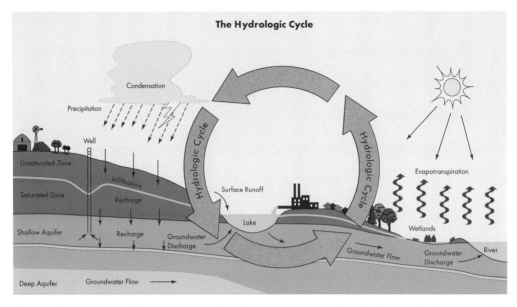

The circulation patterns of freshwater across the planet are known as the hydrologic cycle, because multiple events—precipitation, evaporation, condensation, other forms of transport, and groundwater movement—all occur in a continuous cycle of change. While the total amount of freshwater on Earth remains around 3 percent, this water frequently moves through multiple states, including the precipitation of rain, gaseous vapor formed through evaporation, water delivery through transport in rivers, groundwater movement due to topography and gravity, and being locked in a frozen state such as glaciers or polar ice.

surface of the plants as condensation. Transpiration resembles the reverse of condensation. Moving air evaporates water droplets on plants, and the liquid moisture is turned into a gas.

Temperature and weather play key roles in the hydrology of a wetland. In a very hot and dry climate, such as the Sudan in northeastern Africa, strong winds cause rapid evaporation and therefore limit the existence of wetland areas. Compare this to a cool and moist location, such as northern Sweden, where water-loving plant species thrive due to a rainy climate and slower evaporation rates.

Both freshwater and saltwater wetlands rely on the periodic inflow of considerable amounts of water to inundate their soils and vegetation. This process brings sediment, nutrients, and organic matter to the wetland and also removes excess water.

In saltwater estuaries, substantial flooding occurs with regular tidal action, up to twice a day. Tidal changes can range from a few inches in the Gulf of Mexico, where the water is very shallow, to as much as 40 feet (12 meters) in the Bay of Fundy in eastern Canada, where a deep estuary is filled and emptied with each tidal action.

Freshwater wetlands that are exposed to considerable inflow from rivers or lakes periodically will be flooded, especially during spring or summer storms.

However, some freshwater wetlands, such as a bog or fen, may be isolated. These biomes may have water levels that fluctuate by only a few inches in a year.

The flow rate, volume, and quality of water play direct roles in a wetland's chemical, biological, and ecological functions. Wetlands also rely on the input of nutrients such as nitrogen and phosphorus to sustain plant and animal growth. Three distinct classifications characterize wetland fertility. A wetland that is oligotrophic (from the Greek words *oligo,* meaning "small," and *trophe,* meaning "food") has waters that are saturated with oxygen but contain little plant and animal life due to lower levels of nutrients. One example is the Rio Negro, located in the northwestern Amazon Rain Forest in Brazil. This water body is dark in color from the dissolved humic acid and tannins from the decay of vegetation. Some bogs with considerable water flow also can be oligotrophic.

A wetland that is mesotrophic (from the Greek word *meso,* meaning "medium") has moderate clarity and levels of nutrients in the water. Thus, it supports a greater density of plant life, including algae and plankton.

This type of wetland became threatened in the late twentieth century by the growing population—mainly nutrient loading due to residential, agricultural, and industrial pollution. When too much nitrogen and phosphorus accumulate in water, algae blooms result, and the excess vegetation consumes all available oxygen, starving fish, other animals, and plant life. Sources of these nutrients include storm water runoff, septic systems, agricultural waste streams, and home/garden runoff. Mesotrophic wetlands still can be found in most fens, especially in the northern latitudes of Canada, Western Europe, Russia, and China.

On the far end of the nutrient-loaded scale, a wetland that is eutrophic (from the Greek word *eutrophos,* meaning "well nourished") has the least flow of water. Due to the extremely high influx of nutrients from a number of sources, including animal and human waste and chemical fertilizers, it features very dense plant and algae growth. Eutrophic wetlands often are found adjacent to agricultural or developed areas.

The process of eutrophication refers to an ecosystem that has become overenriched with nitrogen and phosphorus and develops a low level of oxygen. This is caused by massive plant and algae blooms that consume dissolved oxygen and create an excess of decaying organic material. Such ecosystems often exhibit large amounts of dead fish, or fish kills, in summer months, when the animals expire from the depletion of oxygen in the water. Extra organic matter also creates a blanket of choking material, limiting microbiological activity and threatening the survival of submerged grasses and plants.

One noteworthy area experiencing eutrophication is the Chesapeake Bay. Bordered by Virginia and Maryland, this 4,479-square-mile (11,601-square-kilometer) saltwater habitat is the biggest coastal estuary in the United States. In the 1980s, the bay was found to contain multiple "dead zones," where excessive nutrients had resulted in fish, crab, and clam kills. A regional cleanup effort called the Chesapeake Bay Program has restored some areas, but algae blooms persist.

Today, a significant number of lakes and coastal wetlands around the world are threatened due to eutrophication. These include 54 percent of such waterways in Asia, 53 percent in Europe, 41 percent in South America, and 28 percent in Africa.

Examples of Wetland Systems

A wetland can range in size from a backyard ditch to a watershed stretching hundreds of square miles and containing several types of smaller wetlands. Wetlands are present on every continent on Earth, from the hottest to the coldest climates. Three examples of distinct wetlands from around the world help show the resource's diversity, in terms of both geographical and ecological conditions.

The Mekong River

The Mekong River in Southeast Asia, the twelfth-longest river in the world, is 2,600 miles (4,183 kilometers) long. It includes a watershed area greater than 300,000 square miles (770,000 square kilometers). Along the Mekong are a number of freshwater and saltwater marshes, mangrove swamps, and other types of swamps, spanning portions of Tibet, China, the Union of Myanmar (formerly Burma), Laos, Vietnam, and Cambodia.

More than thirty years after the Vietnam War ended, the region is experiencing regrowth of aquatic vegetation in the Mekong mangrove swamps that lost up to 480 square miles (1,243 square kilometers) of wetlands due to the use of Agent Orange, a chemical herbicide and defoliant deployed from U.S. military aircraft to reduce forest ground cover. Today, Mekong River mangrove swamps contain up to sixty species of trees, forty species of mammals, and 200 bird species.

Because 40 percent of the area's population lives within the immediate river basin, however, very few wetlands have remained undisturbed by human activity. And while human and agricultural pollution has degraded water quality in larger towns and cities, the biggest threat to the river's stability (and adjacent wetlands) is a series of proposed hydroelectric dams. The intended benefits of the 100 planned dams include an increase in electricity and more agricultural irrigation opportunities using impounded water. However, construction of the dams—a dozen had been built as of 2009—has limited ecologically beneficial flooding, reduced freshwater flows to wetland mangroves and the delta where the river meets the South China Sea, and cut off native fish migration from the lower to the upper river.

The Niger River

The Niger River in West Africa contains up to 120,000 square miles (310,800 square kilometers) of freshwater wetlands and 4,000 square miles (10,360 square kilometers) of saltwater mangroves where it drains into the Gulf of Guinea and the Atlantic Ocean. These wetlands host a diversity of wildlife, including crocodiles, elephants, hippopotamuses, and manatees.

Flood season, which lasts from July to October, sees the river's banks spill over to form what becomes almost an inland sea at the delta, although many areas are shallow and less than a foot deep. As the water recedes, farmers move their cattle from dry areas to wet ones and establish new crops. This action often disturbs seasonal wetlands.

The Nigerian government attempts to limit damage by regulating wetland use, but as the dry season hits its peak, herders of goats, the region's most common livestock, cut live wetland trees and bushes to feed their animals. Recognizing the importance of the wetlands in supporting their fisheries and the wetland ecosystem, local tribal leaders have been discouraging cutting wetland vegetation, and offenders caught breaking this mandate must pay fines.

The Mississippi River

The Mississippi River travels 2,320 miles (6,009 kilometers) from start to finish and drains into a coastal estuary that contains up to 40 percent of all the coastal wetlands in the lower forty-eight United States. At the end of its journey, the longest river in North America features distinctive bottomland hardwood wetlands that line its distinctive floodplains. These wetlands rely on regular storms delivering water and sediment to nourish their soils and grow vegetation.

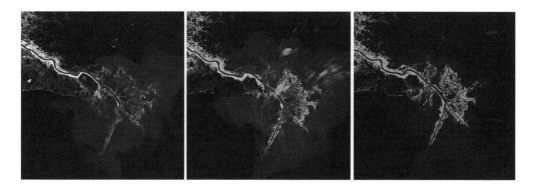

These images, taken in 1973, 1989, and 2003, show changes in the delta of the Mississippi River in Louisiana. The delta marks where the river ends, and a fan-shaped deposit of sediments is visible at the beginning of the Gulf of Mexico. Factors such as wetland removal have caused the area of sediment accumulation to shrink, allowing for the intrusion of salt water into freshwater habitats. *(United States Geological Survey)*

Human-engineered changes to the river—intended to control periodic flooding and alter boat navigation courses in order to enhance commercial barge traffic—have resulted in a dramatic reduction in water flow and sediment deposited in wetland areas. These changes have led to a loss of 7,000 square miles (18,130 square kilometers) of wetlands since the 1970s.

Part of the devastation caused by Hurricane Katrina in Louisiana and Mississippi in 2005 was due to a reduction in wetlands from removals, dredging, channel alteration, and other development projects. This work substantially affected the ability of the Mississippi River wetlands and other coastal areas to provide a buffer for inland areas and absorb the storm surge of floodwaters.

Wetland Inventories

Not until 1999 was a worldwide inventory of wetlands undertaken. Previously, governments and scientific organizations had conducted inventories only for countries or single continents. The first global assessment was performed by a collaboration of organizations, including the Secretariat of the Convention on Wetlands (created in Ramsar, Iran, in 1971), Wetlands International (a private, nonprofit scientific research organization based in the Netherlands), and the British government. Their report found a total of 6.5 billion acres (2.6 billion hectares) of wetlands across the planet, or 10 million square miles (26 square kilometers), an area approximately the size of North America.

This 1999 inventory also estimated the types of wetlands in existence, but only classified 4 billion acres (1.6 billion hectares) of the 6.5 billion acres (2.6 billion hectares) identified, due to a lack of aerial and satellite mapping or reliable field data. It estimated that the majority of wetlands identified were saltwater wetlands or freshwater marshes (2.3 billion acres, or 931 million hectares), followed by agricultural wetlands (321 million acres, or 130 million hectares) and coral reef wetlands (148 million acres, or 60 million hectares).

The study was critical of the varying assessment methods used around the world to classify wetlands, separate databases maintained by different entities, and the lack of funding available to complete an in-depth assessment. Although the United States and parts of Europe periodically undertook thorough inventories, most nations lacked reliable and up-to-date information.

Wetlands in the United States have been intensively mapped and studied. In 1906, the U.S. Department of Agriculture conducted the first national wetland inventory to identify areas to be converted to farmland. In 1954, the U.S. Geological Survey and the U.S. Fish and Wildlife Service completed the first inventory for the purpose of conservation. The 1954 results found a total of

WETLAND AMOUNTS IN THE UNITED STATES, 2006

LOWER STATES (including Hawaii)

Saltwater Wetlands	Percent (%)	Size (Acres)
Marshes/Estuaries	73	3 million
Nonvegetated	14	0.7 million
Shrub Wetlands	13	0.7 million
Total (5% national amount):		4.4 million

Freshwater Wetlands		
Forested Wetlands	51	51.4 million
Marshes	25	26.2 million
Shrub Wetlands	17	18.5 million
Nonvegetated	3	5.9 million
Wetland Ponds	6	5.5 million
Total (95% national amount):		107.5 million

ALASKA		
Saltwater Wetlands		2.1 million
Freshwater Wetlands		171.9 million
Total (Alaska):		174 million

Source: U.S. Fish and Wildlife Service, National Wetlands Inventory Program.

74 million acres (30 million hectares) of wetlands across the country, excluding Alaska. States with the largest wetland areas were Florida (17 million acres, or 7 million hectares), Georgia (5 million acres, or 2 million hectares), North Carolina (4 million acres, or 1.6 million hectares), Texas (3 million acres, or 1.2 million hectares), and South Carolina (3 million acres, or 1.2 million hectares).

In 1975, the U.S. Fish and Wildlife Service began new mapping efforts, and in 1986, the U.S. Congress passed the Emergency Wetlands Resources Act, which directed the service to establish a National Wetlands Inventory Program. Since then, the inventory work has produced 50,800 maps covering 88 percent of the lower forty-eight states and 30 percent of Alaska.

As of 2006, there were 107.5 million acres (43.5 million hectares) of wetlands in the conterminous United States, making up 5.5 percent of the country's total surface area. An inventory of Alaska wetlands recorded 174 million acres (70 million hectares) of wetlands, nearly 51 percent of that state's landmass.

In 2008, after nearly three centuries of wetlands losses, the U.S. Fish and Wildlife Service announced a net gain of 1.1 million acres (0.4 million hectares) of new wetland areas. Almost all of the increase was in freshwater areas, due to cooperative efforts with farmers and restoration of industrial sites.

Biodiversity of Wetlands

Scientists estimate that, next to rain forests, wetlands are the most prolific and productive ecosystems in the world. This productivity is due to the fact that many wetland organisms have the ability to capture the sun's energy and carry out photosynthesis to create usable, chemical energy. For example, the cattail (*Typha latifolia*), which lives in freshwater marshes, can produce up to 12 tons (24,000 pounds, or 10,886 kilograms) of biomass in a single acre in one growing season. This organic output rivals that of enriched agricultural land.

Biodiversity is defined as the variability of life-forms at all levels within an ecosystem, and it often is associated with an ecosystem's biological health. Wetlands contain an impressive inventory of animal and plant life, including birds, both waterfowl and other species; invertebrates, such as plankton, snails, worms, insects, spiders, and jellyfish; reptiles, such as turtles and alligators; amphibians, such as frogs and salamanders; and mammals, such as beavers, muskrats, and mice. There are more than 20,000 species of fish in the world, and 8,500 of them, or 40 percent, live in freshwater wetlands. There are more than 4,000 species of amphibians on the planet, with more than 60 percent living in wetlands.

East Africa

Substantial wetland biodiversity can be found in a series of lakes in East Africa, called the Rift Valley Lakes, which include Lake Malawi, Lake Tanganyika, and Lake Victoria and are spread across portions of the Democratic Republic of the Congo, Kenya, Rwanda, Tanzania, and Uganda. Formed by a 4,000-mile-long (6,436-kilometer-long) geologic rift, this chain of up to a dozen bodies of water features some of the continent's most diverse freshwater wetlands, with millions of acres supporting water-dependent species.

One spectacular body of water is Lake Tanganyika. At 418 miles (673 kilometers) long and 31 miles (50 kilometers) wide, it is Africa's second-largest freshwater body; at 4,850 feet (1,478 meters), it is the second-deepest lake in the world. Scientific studies have revealed a unique diversity of wetland species living along the expansive marsh ecosystem of Lake Tanganyika, including up to 500 species that are endemic to the area. Scientists have documented 400 species of fish and 737 types of amphibians in and around these waters.

Mangrove trees such as this one in Australia help stabilize the wetlands they grow in. The roots protect coastal areas from soil erosion by dissipating wave energy, as well as by slowing the flow of tidal water so that soil deposits remain after the tide ebbs. (© EcoView/Fotolia)

Australia

Another example of wetland diversity can be found in Australia, where much of the continent is arid or semi-arid with little rainfall. These conditions directly limit the number and size of wetlands. In coastal regions, native species have adapted to unique chemical conditions, such as high salinity (greater than 75 parts per thousand). For instance, one species of endemic brine shrimp (*Paratemia zietziana*) can live in saltwater conditions of up to 300 parts per thousand, thriving alongside vegetation that has similar tolerance.

Along Australia's northern, eastern, and western coasts, expansive mangroves and marshes exceed 4,500 square miles (11,665 square kilometers). These wetlands support twenty-five species of frogs, up to sixty species of waterbirds, more than 100 species of fish, and in excess of 20,000 insect species. One of the more interesting species here is the platypus (*Ornithorhynchus anatinus*), a venomous, duck-billed aquatic mammal that lays eggs instead of giving birth to live young.

Canadian Northwest Territories

The Canadian Northwest Territories occupy a region spanning 440,479 square miles (1.1 million square kilometers), from the edge of the Arctic Ocean southward for 1,000 miles (1,609 kilometers). The territories contain a high density of freshwater wetland habitats, including peat bogs, floodplains, marshes, and wet tundra, and encompassing nearly 25 percent of the area. Much of this landscape is treeless due to low-nutrient soil, excessive moisture, and cold winter temperatures.

These subarctic, boreal, mountain, and prairie wetlands host a rich diversity of species, including the trumpeter swan (*Cygnus buccinator*) and the whooping crane (*Grus Americana*), two rare large birds that thrive in North American water habitats, feeding on primarily submerged wetland vegetation. An abundant variety of wetland grasses, sedges, rushes, and shrubs provide excellent habitat for a waterfowl population that is estimated at 150,000 swans, 6 million geese, and 62 million ducks. In the summer season, up to twenty-four species of shore birds nest in the northern Fraser River Delta, exceeding 1 million individuals in a given year.

These areas also are occupied by twelve species of mammals, such as American mink (*Neovison vison*) and North American moose (*Alces alces*); twelve species of reptiles, such as garter snakes (*Thamnophis sirtalis*) and snapping turtles (*Chelydra serpentina*); thirteen species of amphibians, such as spring peepers (*Pseudacris cruicifer*) and American bullfrogs (*Rana catesbeiana*); 150 species of fish, such as northern pike (*Esox lucius*) and walleye (*Sander vitreus*); and hundreds of species of invertebrates, such as northern crayfish (*Orconectes virilis*) and mussels (*Epioblasma torulosa*).

Selected Web Sites

Australian Wetlands Group: http://www.wetlandcare.com.au.
Ramsar Convention on Wetlands: http://www.ramsar.org.
U.S. Fish and Wildlife Service National Wetlands Inventory: http://www.fws.gov/nwi/.
United Nations Environment Programme: http://www.unep.or.jp.
Wetlands of Ontario: http://www.on.ec.gc.ca/wetlands/.

Further Reading

Batzer, Darold, ed. *Ecology of Freshwater and Estuarine Wetlands.* Berkeley: University of California Press, 2007.

Gilman, Kevin. *Hydrology and Wetland Conservation.* New York: John Wiley and Sons, 2004.

Mitsch, William, and James G. Gosselink. *Wetlands.* Hoboken, NJ: John Wiley and Sons, 2007.

Moore, Peter. *Wetlands.* New York: Facts on File, 2001.

U.S. Fish and Wildlife Service. *Status and Trends of Wetlands in the Conterminous United States.* Washington, DC: U.S. Department of the Interior, 2005.

Van Der Valk, Arnold. *The Biology of Freshwater Wetlands.* New York: Oxford University Press, 2006.

Ward, Andy. *Environmental Hydrology.* Boca Raton, FL: Lewis, 2006.

3 | Humans and Wetlands

Since ancient times, humankind's relationship with wetlands has been complex and varied. Human use of and synergy with wetlands dates back tens of thousands of years to the earliest agricultural settlements.

Many wetlands that people have used in the past no longer exist due to succession (natural change in the composition of an ecosystem), or landform alterations due to volcanic activity, earthquakes, erosion, flooding, sea level changes, or glacial processes. Many that do exist contain evidence of communities that once thrived in these complex ecosystems and provide historians and scientists alike with information on social units, agricultural methods, and related economic systems.

Still other current wetlands host examples of modern-day communities living in partnership with wetlands. Factors such as population growth, industrial and agricultural development, governmental programs aimed at reducing and/or eliminating wetlands, and twentieth- and twenty-first century wetland conservation efforts all play a role in the history and future of wetlands.

Ancient Sites and Cultures

Although numerous ancient cultures and their respective communities have been lost to history, three wetland environments in particular reveal distinct communities that lived and thrived in these ecosystems. Evidence of these societies often has been preserved in wetland soils, where low oxygen and bacteria essentially halted decomposition of organic materials.

ECONOMIC BENEFITS OF WETLANDS

Action	Goal
Environmental protection	Habitat for biodiversity, water filtration, storm protection, carbon sink, oxygen gas producer, and nutrient supplier.
Fill, draining	Farming, building, and mining.
Forest resources	Wood for fuel and construction.
Hydrologic changes	Flood control, boat navigation, and water removal.
Mining	Minerals, precious materials, and metals.
Peat bog mining	Fuel, farming, and gardening.

Source: U.S. Environmental Protection Agency, 2006.

Lough Boora Parklands

Ireland's Lough Boora Parklands contain some of the world's oldest evidence of human use of wetlands, dating from around 6800 B.C.E., the Mesolithic Period. The Parklands hold thousands of acres of peat bog wetlands spanning eleven counties and three provinces in County Offaly in the Irish midlands. Prior to the discovery of the Lough Boora site, archaeologists believed that the first human settlements were near Ireland's coast and that the midlands remained unsettled in the Mesolithic Period.

Excavations in 1977 found evidence that the people who lived here harvested the wetland's peat for fuel and insulation and that they used the wood from its trees for buildings and fires. Studies of the soil have shown that settlers also intentionally burned sections of wetland at intervals, a technique used to improve the productivity of cultivated areas, reduce vegetation height, and improve conditions for hunting where wildlife gathered.

Other evidence has revealed food-processing areas, toolmaking stations, and basic camps used by small groups of residents. In addition, scientists have uncovered black stone tools made of chert, a rock similar to flint, in glacial deposits.

Biskupin

Another example of early wetlands use dates to around 720 B.C.E. in Biskupin (present-day Poland) in north-central Europe. This settlement contained nearly 1,000 Lusatians, an Indo-European indigenous people.

Living on a peninsula in a freshwater marsh, members of this highly organized society strategically utilized the wetlands to build a complex fort-like structure. Residents constructed thirteen rows of uniform houses from nearby oak trees and used the adjacent wetland water for irrigation and drinking. They added wetland soils as nutrients to gardens planted throughout the compound and grew species of wheat, as well as barley and Celtic beans. Scientists believe the settlement was destroyed by attack, fire, or flood, but evidence of it was preserved in the wetland mud.

Archeologists discovered the site in 1933. Their excavations developed into the largest venture in the history of Polish archaeology. Archaeologists and conservators continue to work to protect and preserve the structures, as changes in underground water levels threaten to oxidize and damage those timber structures that are still underground. The Archeological Museum in Biskupin has overseen the construction of the replica's fortress components on-site to demonstrate the impressive accomplishments of the Lusatians.

Yucatán Peninsula

The Yucatán Peninsula in northern Central America features a network of freshwater wetlands that were used by the Maya people around 100 B.C.E. Archeological evidence shows that a population of several thousand lived adjacent to wetlands in the northeastern part of the peninsula. The Maya raked nutrient-rich submerged soils into their agricultural rows to enrich crop production, redirected water with an irrigation system of sophisticated gravity-fed, hand-dug channels, and cut wetland plant and tree species with durable characteristics to make building materials and tools.

The Mayan population was dramatically reduced after the Spanish colonized the region in the early sixteenth century. In addition, weather pattern shifts resulted in significant drying of the climate, which led to changes in native lifeways. Twenty-first-century scientific and economic discussions have focused on ways to return the local Mexican and Guatemalan populations to some of the ancient Mayan practices in order to enhance the agricultural sustainability of the region.

Modern Communities

There are several present-day communities that effectively use wetlands to their benefit with little impact on the ecology of the area. Their agricultural practices, which include rotating crops and channeling floodwaters for irrigation, show that a mutual relationship is sustainable as long as nutrient and waste inputs are balanced and polluted water is treated or removed on a consistent basis.

The Zambezi River Population

The Zambezi River originates in northwestern Zambia, a southern African country with regions rich in waterfalls, mountains, and rain forests. Together with its tributaries, the Zambezi forms the fourth-largest river basin of the African continent.

From 1800 B.C.E., the Upper Zambezi and associated wetlands have played a central role in supporting the rural economy of the area. Springtime annual floods from the river create a roughly 60- to 175-mile (97- to 282-kilometer) tract full of floodplains that disperse water, sediment, and nutrients to the seasonal wetlands and lowlands.

One group of native peoples demonstrates a unique and respectful relationship to the wetlands. The Lozi (whose name translates as "plain," referring to the open terrain of their homeland) live along the river in the Barotse Province of western Zambia. Over thousands of years, the Lozi have developed a series of sustainable agricultural practices. Their crops and methods vary with the location of the plot, the type of soil, the amount of moisture in the air, and the population's current needs.

Each year when the lowlands flood, the Lozi move their villages to higher ground. Once the water recedes, they return to plant their crops of cassava, bulrush millet, maize, rice, and sorghum. They maintain basic canals to channel floodwaters to irrigate their crops. Whatever water is not absorbed runs off, either through the surface or underground and returns to the Zambezi.

Chinese Wetland Harvesters

China, a nation of approximately 1.5 billion people, or 22 percent of the world's population, has 304 million acres (123 million hectares) of arable land, or 0.23 acres (0.09 hectares) per capita, which is less than 40 percent of the world's average. In order to increase food production in a country with limited farmland, the government has historically permitted the removal of wetlands and the widespread use of chemical pesticides, herbicides, and fertilizers.

In a more sustainable approach, the rural residents of Guangdong Province in southern China have used aquaculture, the controlled farming of freshwater and saltwater species, within wetlands for hundreds of years. This includes crops of fish, mollusks, crustaceans, and aquatic plants. Wetlands occupy 21 percent of the landmass in this southern subtropical climate, and the area hosts 1,314 different streams and tributaries that converge at the wetland delta where it meets the sea. This 50-square-mile (130-square-kilometer) area of coastal estuaries offers a diverse saltwater habitat for up to 201 species of birds, 181 species of

Fish farms in China supply about 70 percent of the fish farmed in the world. Unfortunately, these agricultural sites recently have been plagued with contaminated freshwater laden with sewage, industrial waste, and pesticides. In 2007, the U.S. refused seafood from these farms forty-three times due to chemical contamination. In one example, eel shipments were refused because farmers used nitrofuran to kill high bacteria levels in order to keep fish alive until they were packaged for sale. This drug is a known cancer-causing agent and is banned in the United States in relation to animal husbandry. *(© Waimong/Fotolia)*

plants, sixty-two species of reptiles, forty types of amphibians, and twenty-eight species of mammals.

In these nutrient-rich waters, farmers utilize extensive lagoon systems to simultaneously hold fish and crustaceans and to grow plants along the edges of the water. They monitor soil chemistry and carefully manage water drainages to avoid too much nutrient content, high water temperatures, or stranding their crops. In an effort to encourage the efficient use of land, the Chinese government has awarded subsidies to farmers in this area who have modified their aquaculture—for instance, by combining crops such as baby clams with mud snails to improve yields and reduce water pollution.

Klamath Basin Farmers

The 50-by-70-mile (80-by-113-kilometer) Klamath Basin straddles the border between California and Oregon in the western United States. This wetlands-rich basin became very popular for farming at the beginning of the twentieth century. Over decades, however, efforts to fill wetlands, overuse of water, and pollution resulted in the loss of up to 75 percent of the local wetlands.

In response to this loss and in an effort to preserve what remains of this valuable ecosystem, the federal government designated six federal National Wildlife Refuges between 1908 and 1978. These protected areas encompass 186,181 acres (75,345 hectares) of wetlands and open water, supporting 433 species of wildlife, including up to 6 million waterfowl.

In 2006, farmers paid $1.43 million per year to use 15,500 acres (6,273 hectares) of this land. In return, the farmers and the agricultural community at large have agreed to abide by strict environmental controls. Practices applied to enhance the long-term health of the wetlands include rotating crops, limiting water removal, and reducing the addition of nutrients and pesticides.

Crops, including alfalfa, onions, and potatoes, are bountiful in the rich floodplain soils. Farmers rely on the periodic flooding of lowlands to limit soil diseases and insect infestations. The flooding reduces the need for soil pesticides, saving each farmer up to $200 an acre per year. Agricultural output increased by nearly 25 percent between 2002 and 2006 under this cooperative program between the public and private sectors.

Population Growth Impacts on Wetlands

The considerable global population growth since the early 1800s resulted in extensive residential, industrial, and agricultural development. This development, often occurring near water resources, correlates with wetland losses.

The planet's population grew from 978 million people in 1800 to 6.7 billion in 2009. According to the Population Reference Bureau, which is based in Washington, D.C., the world's population growth in 2009 was 82.8 million people. Up to 70 percent of the population lives in coastal regions, putting enormous pressure on coastal wetlands.

As more people have filled more communities, they have expanded into lowlands and wetlands. Their economies required resource consumption, leading to wetland destruction and degradation of water quality from pollution. Even though the three major industrial regions—Western Europe, North America, and Asia—developed differently over time, similar activities in each location have resulted in widespread damage to diverse wetland habitats.

Western Europe

Heavy European wetland losses began in the 1400s, when engineered water diversion systems were built in Britain, France, and Germany to support larger cities. By 1750, Europe had 163 million residents. By 1900, the population of Europe had more than doubled to 410 million.

During the Industrial Revolution (about 1700 to 1900), factories often were built next to open water or wetlands, which served as water sources and drainage sites. By 1993, it was estimated that dredging, filling, draining, and altering had eliminated 50 percent of wetlands in Europe, including those in Germany, Greece, Italy, The Netherlands, Portugal, Spain, and the United Kingdom.

Peat bogs were especially damaged, with losses exceeding 55 percent in eleven countries. In France, up to 66 percent of the nation's historic wetlands were lost between 1900 and 1993. In the United Kingdom, 52 percent of freshwater marshes were lost between 1947 and 1982 due to programs that allowed drainage for farm expansions. Scotland lost up to 23 percent of its lowland mires due to unregulated peat removals.

By 1999, the population of Europe had surpassed 729 million residents. An inventory in 2001 by Wetlands International estimated that 11 percent of Europe contained wetlands, covering approximately 1 million square miles (3 million square kilometers). Continued growth of the population to 830 million by 2009 places great pressure on wetlands protection efforts in the twenty-first century.

North America

Between 1780 and 1980, the North American population grew from 82 million to 256 million people, a threefold increase. During this time, westward expansion across the middle of the United States resulted in new farming communities in regions where prairie potholes were common. These small wetlands left over from glacial activity dominated the landscape and supported an enormous waterfowl population historically estimated at more than 100 million birds.

Nearly 53 percent of U.S. wetlands (excluding those in Alaska) were lost during this 200-year period. The states of California and Ohio altered 90 percent of their native wetlands. In contrast, Alaska, which was sparsely populated, lost only 1 percent of its wetlands.

Much of the wetland losses in the lower forty-eight states was due to two factors: urban/suburban growth and agricultural expansion. The construction of new houses, factories, and other commercial enterprises in a booming economy resulted in bulldozers removing wetlands, which were assumed to be unsightly, breeders of disease, and an impediment to prosperity.

In the 1950s, larger tractors and better seed and fertilizer technology revolutionized the agricultural profession. An unprecedented expansion of farms began. Increased water needs meant lakes, streams, and brooks were used to irrigate fields, further impacting wetlands across the nation.

Asia

Asia's population and economic growth came later than Western European and North American expansion, not peaking until the twentieth-first century. Historically, Asia employed a more integrated version of agriculture in wetland areas, as exemplified by rice and fish farming in paddies beginning 6,500 years ago.

However, as the East needed to produce more food in the 1960s, the floodplain regions of the continent—including the Red River in Vietnam, to cite one example—were almost completely removed. Widespread river diversions to get water to fields and to supply the big cities left wetland communities heavily altered. Examples of wetlands that endured almost two centuries of negative human impacts included the Yangtze and Yellow rivers in China, the Klang and Gombak rivers in Malaysia, and the Ping River in Thailand. Wetland losses since 1800 vary by country: Thailand, 82 percent; Malaysia, 71 percent; Indonesia, 18 percent; and China, 13 percent.

When China's population reached 1 billion people in 1983, economic demand for food resulted in the adoption of Western farming practices and considerable crop growth. This dramatically quickened the pace of wetland losses in China. It still continues at a rate of up to 1.2 million (500,000 hectares) acres per year.

Government's Role in Wetland Destruction

Throughout history, multiple geographic and cultural depictions have portrayed wetlands as inhospitable, unsafe, and sources of deadly diseases such as malaria and yellow fever. These portrayals were based on uninformed opinions and fear rather than knowledge and science. However, governments around the world, seeking to protect the public and failing to recognize the ecological value of wetlands, have funded projects that have resulted in hundreds of square miles of wetland losses.

As the world's population surged between the nineteenth and twenty-first centuries, the public infrastructure for commercial and industrial facilities, as

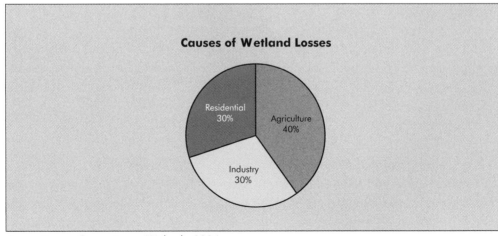

Source: Ramsar Convention on Wetlands, 2004.

well as residential communities, often was placed in areas where freshwater sources were abundant. Numerous roads, bridges, factories, and other buildings were constructed on wetlands, resulting in the loss of 30 percent of global wetlands.

Economic and Agricultural Expansion

Three examples chronicle the detrimental impacts to wetlands across two continents. The first began in the late 1800s in northern Germany. At the time, the floodplains and wetlands of the Rhine River became the focus of a massive effort to grow the economy. With government funding and approval, numerous factories were constructed that polluted the Rhine. Wetlands also were demolished when the government straightened or widened the course of the river to allow for ship and barge transport of materials to these sites. Three generations of government engineers worked to implement a plan to drain entire floodplains between the cities of Karlsruhe and Basel, removing several thousand acres of wetlands in the process.

In order to make sure citizens have enough food, governments often support the conversion of wetlands into farmland, a process that has resulted in approximately 40 percent of historic wetland losses. In Pakistan, for example, a massive government effort was undertaken in the 1950s to help sustain the rapidly expanding population. Greater than 70 percent of the Indus River was diverted to create new agricultural areas, leaving only 30 percent of the original flow to support 2,300 square miles (5,957 square kilometers) of wetlands.

By 1992, the Pakistani government had constructed sixteen large dams, three massive reservoirs, and a system of three dozen canals totaling more than 35,000 miles (56,315 kilometers) in length. Although this construction successfully diverted freshwater to the farming industry and facilitated feeding up to 100 million people, the program also resulted in saline damage—mineral-laden water resulted in salt accumulation in soils, reducing the area's available cropland by 150 square miles (389 square kilometers) per year. In addition, the rare freshwater dolphin (*Platanista minor*), indigenous to the Indus River, has become threatened due to water pollution and wetland habitat loss.

One of the best orchestrated efforts by a government agency to reduce wetlands was performed by the U.S. Department of Agriculture, authorized in 1850 by the U.S. Congress in the Swamplands Act. The agency offered incentives to private citizens to convert public wetlands to land under private ownership that could be used primarily for farming. Under this plan, more than 21,000 acres (8,498 hectares) of old-growth Atlantic white cedar (*Chamaecyparis thyoides*) forests were leveled across a wetland area known as the Meadowlands in northern New Jersey. While the government allowed some of the wood to be used for building materials, much of it was burned on-site. In total, 85 million acres (34.4 million hectares) of wetlands were destroyed nationally under this federal program during a 122-year period.

Residential Expansion

The construction of new residential properties often has involved clearing land to maximize the number of developable lots. Flat, dry land means more houses can be built per acre. Wetlands have been filled in by private companies and government entities in order to make space for such new structures. Overall, residential development has destroyed up to 30 percent of the world's wetlands.

In the South American country of Argentina, the city of Buenos Aires sits at the confluence of the Atlantic Ocean, the Parana River, and the Paraguay River. As the population of the city has grown to 12.4 million residents, so have the neighborhoods that encroach on the wetland floodplains. The government funded the construction of hundreds of housing units in these floodplains. City roads and utilities were built to access these areas and to accommodate Buenos Aires's growth. In all, more than 900 square miles (2,331 square kilometers) of wetlands were eliminated to make space for new residential buildings.

Wetland Protection Emerges

The emergence of advanced mechanical technology in the twentieth century resulted in new inventions and improved designs in the form of larger bulldozers, stronger power saws, bigger pumps, deeper drilling rigs, and more powerful hydraulic equipment. This equipment accelerated the pace of wetland removals worldwide. One person with a backhoe could do in a day what had previously taken ten men and a team of horses a week to complete.

The ecological impact of these activities soon became evident in clear-cut forests, altered rivers and streams, drained bogs, filled floodplains, and lower aquifer levels. While developers and others involved in building projects enjoyed short-term economic success, many natural landscapes were adversely impacted.

By the 1960s, the public began to notice the impact of wetland decimation, including increasingly polluted waterways, more erosion, weakened protection from storm flooding, and fewer fish, birds, and other wildlife. Public concern resulted in government and private examination of the causes of and solutions to these pressing ecological issues. As a result, scientists and environmentalists of the 1970s brought forth a new message: Wetlands are valuable as natural resources and as assets, and they should be protected.

The Massachusetts Wetlands Protection Act

The Massachusetts Wetlands Protection Act of 1963 was the first law in the United States to protect wetlands. This legislation made it illegal to alter coastal wetland resource areas without written approval from the state of Massachusetts's environmental protection department. The act aimed to protect the state's public and private drinking water and groundwater supply; control flooding; prevent storm damage and pollution; and preserve fisheries, land containing shellfish, and other wildlife habitats. Massachusetts also was the first state to instill the concept of a buffer zone around a wetland area, so that any work in or within 100 feet (30 meters) of the resource is strictly regulated. The state also allowed towns to further enhance wetland protections—many communities passed their own companion wetland bylaws, practically halting projects within 50 feet of a resource area.

The Ramsar Convention

In 1971, the first intergovernmental treaty for conserving wetlands was signed. The Convention on Wetlands, signed in Ramsar, Iran, and popularly called the Ramsar Convention, provides the framework for national action and international cooperation for the conservation and wise use of wetlands and their resources.

The Ramsar Convention entered into force in 1975, after being ratified by the seventh country, Greece. By 2009, it had 158 contracting parties, or member states, from every corner of the globe. Though the Ramsar Convention's central message is the need for the sustainable use of all wetlands, member states have developed a List of Wetlands of International Importance (termed the "Ramsar List") that designates more than 1,822 key wetlands spanning 656,373 square miles (1.67 million square kilometers), an area larger than the surface area of France, Germany, Spain, and Switzerland combined.

The treaty identifies twenty-five different types of worldwide wetlands (eleven saltwater and fourteen freshwater). When countries join the Ramsar Convention, they are enlisting in an international effort to ensure the conservation and wise use of these unique ecosystems.

The Ramsar Convention Secretariat carries out the day-to-day coordination of the Convention's activities. Located in the headquarters of the World Conservation Union in Gland, Switzerland, the Secretariat has used the treaty's international recognition to develop a strong endowment. The Ramsar Convention has influenced the creation of dozens of additional wetland protection laws and regulations worldwide.

Clean Water Act

Another noteworthy shift toward wetland protection occurred in the United States seventy-three years after the federal government first embarked on wetland management by passing the 1899 Rivers and Harbors Act. In 1972, changes were made to an existing federal water pollution law, giving the federal government significant power to protect wetlands for the first time in its history. Until this point, the focus of environmental laws had been on permitting resource alterations.

The 1972 law was intended, in part, to reduce wetland losses from unpermitted activities by limiting waterway channel construction, wetland filling, and large-scale water-control projects, such as dams and levees. Signed by President Richard M. Nixon after the U.S. Congress overrode his veto, the Water Pollution Control Act, also known as the Clean Water Act, limits any type of discharge into or alteration of a wetland area without a permit. Applicants are notified that if work is conducted they are required to either avoid all wetland areas or mitigate any negative environmental impacts. Depending on scale and location, permits are reviewed by either the U.S. Environmental Protection Agency (EPA), the U.S. Army Corps of Engineers, or a state-authorized agency.

In addition to providing regulatory protection for wetlands, the EPA functions in partnership with state and local governments, the private sector, and citizen organizations to monitor, protect, and restore wetlands. In conjunction with other federal agencies—including the U.S. Fish and Wildlife Service, the U.S. Department of Agriculture, and the National Marine Fisheries Service—the EPA works to mitigate development affecting wetlands, provide incentive for the construction of replacement wetlands, improve water quality, reduce erosion and floods, and protect the biodiversity of wetland habitats. The Clean Water Act was substantially revised in 1977, 1987, and 2002.

Leadership in the Wetland Field

Since the late twentieth century, a network of public and private organizations has formed to advocate for wetland management. Governments in more than 155 countries have drafted wetland laws or regulations that protect both small and large areas. As of 2009, there are more than fifty college programs that specialize in wetland science degrees. This public and private investment in scientific research, educational programs, and the promotion of wetland management and protection has raised public awareness of wetland resource values.

EXCERPT FROM THE CLEAN WATER ACT

FEDERAL WATER POLLUTION CONTROL ACT
(33 U.S.C. 1251 et seq.)
AN ACT To provide for water pollution control activities in the Public Health Service of the Federal Security Agency and in the Federal Works Agency, and for other purposes.

Be it enacted by the Senate and House of Representatives of the United States of America in Congress assembled,

TITLE I—RESEARCH AND RELATED PROGRAMS DECLARATION OF GOALS AND POLICY
SEC. 101. (a) The objective of this Act is to restore and maintain the chemical, physical, and biological integrity of the Nation's waters. In order to achieve this objective it is hereby declared that, consistent with the provisions of this Act—

(1) it is the national goal that the discharge of pollutants into the navigable waters be eliminated by 1985;

(2) it is the national goal that wherever attainable, an interim goal of water quality which provides for the protection and propagation of fish, shellfish, and wildlife and provides for recreation in and on the water be achieved by July 1, 1983;

(3) it is the national policy that the discharge of toxic pollutants in toxic amounts be prohibited;

(4) it is the national policy that Federal financial assistance be provided to construct publicly owned waste treatment works;

(5) it is the national policy that areawide treatment management planning processes be developed and implemented to assure adequate control of sources of pollutants in each State;

(6) it is the national policy that a major research and demonstration effort be made to develop technology necessary to eliminate the discharge of pollutants into the navigable waters, waters of the contiguous zone and the oceans; and

(7) it is the national policy that programs for the control of non-point sources of pollution be developed and implemented in an expeditious manner so as to enable the goals of this Act to be met through the control of both point and non-point sources of pollution.

Wetlands International

The nonprofit group Wetlands International has emerged as a leader in this field. Founded in 1954 as an organization committed to the protection of water-birds, its primary goals include informing the public about the status and health of wetlands, ensuring the functions and values of wetlands are integrated into economic development, and using integrated water management practices to conserve and sustain wetlands.

Based in Wageningen, The Netherlands, with a staff of 150 researchers and educators working in sixteen offices worldwide, the organization has leveraged its global reach by developing a network of up to 1,000 scientists and 15,000 volunteers.

The Society of Wetland Scientists

The Society of Wetland Scientists is an international organization dedicated to promoting knowledge and sustainable use of wetlands. Formed in 1980, it has 3,500 members worldwide. The organization promotes wetland research and management through a science-based approach. A major goal is to use sponsored forums to foster the incorporation of sound science into governmental wetland protection policy. The organization sends out its internationally distributed publication *Wetlands* to several thousand subscribers four times a year.

Based in McLean, Virginia, the society has ten regional offices in the United States. It also has grown into an international organization with chapter offices in Asia, Australia, Europe, and South America.

Ducks Unlimited

Responding to the increased loss of waterfowl in the United States and Canada, Ducks Unlimited was formed in 1937 by hunters and fishermen seeking to conserve wetlands for the purposes of game hunting and fishing. This organization has thrived by supporting grassroots projects that protect wetland habitats, restore wildlife populations, and allow opportunities for continued use, including hunting, fishing, camping, and hiking.

In 2008, Ducks Unlimited directed 88 percent of its resources to conservation programs, and it has conserved 12.6 million acres (5.1 million hectares) of waterfowl habitat in North America since its founding. By 2008, this organization had grown to 780,000 members and, in that year alone, raised $261 million to conserve an additional 300,000 acres (121,406 hectares) of wetlands.

Mitigating Wetland Losses

Recognizing that future wetland losses are an inevitable outcome of population growth and development, in 1983 the U.S. federal government implemented new regulatory policies to offset these losses. One approach from the U.S. Fish and Wildlife Service involved creating new wetland areas or restoring existing ones through so-called wetland banking programs. Under these programs, if a development permit such as the construction of a new highway was going to result in wetland loss, that project would be required to support the creation of a new wetland either by banking the revenue necessary to create this ecosystem elsewhere or by re-creating a wetland on site.

State and local banking programs mitigated wetland losses for several decades. In 1995, the federal government established a regulatory process for wetland preservation. In order to obtain a Section 404 Clean Water Act permit to damage a federal wetland area, an applicant must agree to pay for so-called compensatory mitigation credits to be used elsewhere by a third party.

Also in 1995, the Commission for the European Community, the executive body of the European Union, composed of one representative from each of the twenty-seven member countries, implemented a "no net loss" policy for wetlands. The policy aimed to prohibit wetlands' further degradation, prescribe their wise use, and restore damaged areas. The Commission endorsed the use of a system of taxes, fees, subsidies, and tradable permits to provide the most flexibility to those seeking to develop a project that would damage a wetland.

In 2002, the U.S. government drafted the National Wetlands Mitigation Action Plan to streamline and improve mitigation practices nationwide. For the first time in U.S. history, multiple agencies—the Department of Agriculture, the Environmental Protection Agency, the Department of Commerce, and the Army Corps of Engineers—worked collaboratively to identify seventeen major tasks to enhance the ecological performance of areas created under compensatory wetland mitigation. This program is expected to reverse years of wetland losses that exceeded 500,000 acres (202,343 hectares) annually between 1985 and 1999. As of 2006, there were 281.5 million acres (113.9 million hectares) of wetlands in the United States. In 2008, the U.S. Fish and Wildlife Service reported mitigation efforts had resulted in a gain of 1.1 million acres (400,000 hectares) of new wetland areas.

By 2007, sixty-two countries around the world had developed similar banking programs and no net loss policies for compensatory wetland mitigation.

Selected Web Sites

Ducks Unlimited: http://www.ducks.org.

Ramsar Convention on Wetlands: http://www.ramsar.org.

Society of Wetland Scientists: http://www.sws.org.

U.S. Environmental Protection Agency Site on Wetlands Mitigation: http://www.epa.gov/owow/wetlands/.

U.S. Library of Congress, Congressional Research Brief, "Wetlands Issues": http://www.ncseonline.org/NLE/CRSreports/03Aug/IB97014.pdf.

U.S. National Wetlands Mitigation Action Plan: http://www.mitigationactionplan.gov.

United Nations State of the World Population: http://www.unfpa.org/swp/swpmain.htm.

Further Reading

Biebighauser, Thomas. *Wetland Drainage, Restoration, and Repair.* Lexington: University Press of Kentucky, 2007.

Bobbink, Roland, ed. *Wetlands: Functioning, Biodiversity Conservation, and Restoration.* New York: Springer, 2006.

Moore, Peter. *Wetlands.* New York: Facts on File, 2001.

Strand, Margaret. *Wetlands Deskbook.* Washington, DC: Environmental Law Institute, 2001.

U.S. Army Corps of Engineers. *National Wetlands Mitigation Action Plan.* Washington, DC: Multiple Agencies (ACOE, NOAA, EPA, FWS, USDA, and FHA), 2002.

U.S. Library of Congress. *Wetland Issues.* Washington, DC: Congressional Research Service, 2003.

United Nations Population Fund. *State of the World Population 2006.* New York: United Nations, 2006.

Wetlands International. *Wetlands International: Annual Review, 2005.* Wageningen, The Netherlands: Wetlands International, 2006.

WETLANDS OF THE WORLD: CASE STUDIES

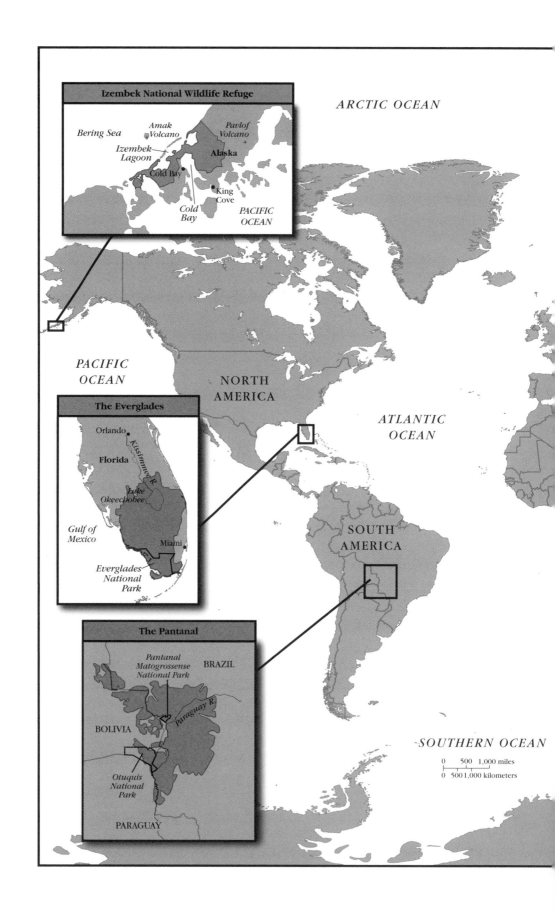

Izembek National Wildlife Refuge

Bering Sea

Amak
Volcano

Pavlof
Volcano

Izembek
Lagoon

Alaska

Cold Bay

King
Cove

Cold
Bay

PACIFIC
OCEAN

ARCTIC OCEAN

PACIFIC
OCEAN

NORTH
AMERICA

ATLANTIC
OCEAN

The Everglades

Orlando

Florida

Kissimmee R.

Lake
Okeechobee

Gulf of
Mexico

Miami

Everglades
National
Park

SOUTH
AMERICA

The Pantanal

Pantanal
Matogrossense
National Park

BRAZIL

Paraguay R.

BOLIVIA

Otuquis
National
Park

PARAGUAY

SOUTHERN OCEAN

0   500   1,000 miles

0   500 1,000 kilometers

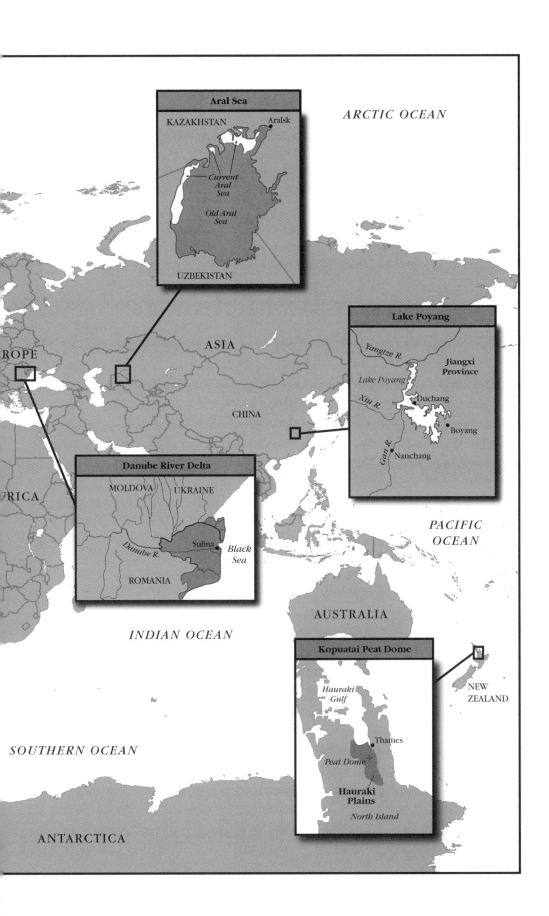

4 Danube River Delta Romania and Ukraine

The Danube River flows from west to east and traverses ten countries in a 1,767-mile (2,843-kilometer) journey from its headwaters in the Black Forest in southwestern Germany to the Black Sea in eastern Romania. As Europe's second-longest river (after Russia's Volga River), its name comes from the ancient Iranian word *danu,* meaning "river."

The Danube River basin is 310,800 square miles (804,972 square kilometers) in size, and it passes along or through Germany, Slovakia, Austria, Hungary, Croatia, Serbia, Romania, Bulgaria, Moldavia, and Ukraine. Before the river empties into the Black Sea, it widens into a triangular-shaped wetland delta of 2,622 square miles (6,791 square kilometers) in area, the equivalent of 1.6 million acres (0.6 million hectares). Europe's largest continuous wetland complex, almost 80 percent of the Danube River Delta is within Romania, and 20 percent is within Ukraine.

The Danube River Delta hosts a maze of freshwater and saltwater marshes, mangrove swamps, and open water. It supports a diversity of plant and animal life, including 1,200 varieties of aquatic and terrestrial plants, 280 bird species, and forty-five freshwater fish species. It is Europe's largest stopover location for bird migrations, with millions of individuals congregating in the spring and fall.

No point of the delta is higher than 30 feet (9 meters) above sea level, and only 9 percent of its area is permanently above water. Known for its extensive marshland, it is dominated by expansive marshes of thin reed grasses and sedges covering 1,042 square miles (2,699 square kilometers), more than half of the total wetland area.

DANUBE DELTA HABITAT TYPES

Lakes	Wet meadows
Flooded islets	Dry meadows
Flooded reeds	Sandy and rocky areas
Riverine forests	Steep banks
Cane fields	Upland forests
Sandy and muddy beaches	

Source: United Nations Environment Program.

Each year, the Danube River carries hundreds of thousands of pounds of sediment and nutrients downriver, depositing much of it in the delta. This process continually changes the footprint of the wetlands. Due to an overabundance of nutrients from farming and toxins from pollution, invasive plants such as the common reed (*Phragmites australis*) thrive in the underwater soils and grow up to 13 feet (4 meters) in height, with fifteen root shoots per square foot.

Four types of sturgeon (belonging to the Genus *Acipenser*) are common fish in the region; however, commercial fishing, pollution, and hydrologic changes have forced two other species of sturgeon (Atlantic sturgeon, *Acipenser sturio,* and ship sturgeon, *Acipenser nudiventris*) to the brink of extinction. The area hosts a healthy tern population, including the sandwich tern (*Thalasseus sandvicensis*) and the black tern (*Chlidonias niger*). Other wildlife includes otters, minks, and a species of wild cat (*Felis sylvestris*) that lives on the islets.

Human Uses

Nearly 15,000 people live within the delta area. The majority, called Lipovans, immigrated two centuries ago from Russia. They settled the lowlands in the 1800s, constructed buildings on pilings to stay above floodwaters, installed complex canals for boat travel, developed expert fishing skills, and cultivated a lifestyle in the wetlands.

In the twenty-first century, however, the human presence in the area has been progressively shrinking due to an aging population and limited economic opportunities. This has meant nearly 50 percent fewer people in the delta since the mid-twentieth century. Residents use the lowlands for farming and cattle grazing, and they primarily fish for sturgeon and carp. Nearly 10,000 boats are registered in the delta. The Romanian town of Sulina is the busiest port with numerous visits from Black Sea commercial fishing boats each day.

Living conditions are poor for some Danube River Delta residents. Traditional seasonal fishing huts, made from reed grass, are rare but still can be found. A handful of communities do not have electricity or phones. And diseases such as cholera occasionally break out, infecting hundreds of people.

The Romanian portion of the delta is managed by the Ministry of the Environment, a government office that enforces conservation laws and maintains waterways. In 1983, to bolster the economy, the Romanian government designated up to 239,000 acres (96,700 hectares) of delta floodplains and wetlands to be converted into farmland. Farms growing grains (such as wheat and barley) and vegetables, as well as vineyards and orchards, were installed by 1987, and another 155,676 acres (63,000 hectares) of wetlands were converted into fish farms shortly thereafter.

Pollution and Damage

The Danube River Delta has experienced significant wetland losses from intensive human activities. Total Danube wetland losses are estimated at greater than 50 percent (1.7 million acres, or 700,000 hectares) as of 2009. Almost 6 percent (3.3 million acres, or 1.3 million hectares) of Romania was covered by wetlands in 1970; by 1999, that number had been cut to less than 3 percent.

Under the twenty-two-year presidency of Nicolae Ceausescu (1967–1989), much of the Romanian delta region was heavily impacted by the development of the commercial fishing and farming industries. In fact, nearly 80 percent of the upper river floodplains and over 69 percent (1,500 square miles, or 3,885 square kilometers) of the delta floodplains have been filled to provide space for such agricultural activities. Additionally, 15 percent (up to 300 square miles, or 777 square kilometers) of the Danube River Delta has been drained entirely.

The Danube River is a major regional transportation channel for cargo shipments. In order to keep the river accessible for larger ships, a number of dredging and river alteration projects were undertaken in the twentieth century. These activities resulted in lost wetlands, reduced water quality, and undermined riverbanks, and they impacted fish and wildlife habitats.

Shipping companies have a considerable presence along the Danube, and they want to remove any impediments to timely commerce, such as shoals, downed trees, or even bends in the river itself. A common Danube commercial shipping industry slogan is, "Adapt the river to the ships, not the ships to the river." Shipping companies assert that the river heals from any damage, as do the fish and wildlife, and they stress that local human livelihoods depend on safe and timely cargo ship travel.

Reduced freshwater flows from an increase in public water withdrawals from the Danube have caused salinity in the delta area to climb from a normal range of 150 milligrams per liter (mg/l) to 350 mg/l; in some places, the salinity has reached a high of 800 mg/l. The delta also periodically receives urban pollution from upriver cities and towns, including toxic pesticides such as DDT (dichlorodiphenyltrichloroethane), used oil products containing dioxins, and high concentrations of metals such as lead and copper. Rural pollution from development and farms includes sediment from erosion and an excess of nutrients such as phosphorus and nitrogen, due to human septic releases, storm water, and farming.

In some cases, these substances have led to the delta's eutrophication, or overenrichment of dissolved nutrients, which has stimulated excessive growth

These pelicans live in the Sulina arm of the Danube Delta in Romania, where they feed on more than forty species of fish, as well as amphibians, crustaceans, and, occasionally, small birds. *(Adrian Silisteanu/AFP/ Getty Images)*

of aquatic plant life such as large algae blooms. The result of these blooms has been the depletion of dissolved oxygen in the water, seasonal fish kills, and an overall reduction in water quality. The summer algae blooms in 1990, for example, forced an entire colony of several thousand pelicans to relocate due to dead fishing grounds.

Farming accounts for 47 percent of land use in the Danube River Basin. Some of the countries along the river—including Bulgaria, Croatia, and Romania—generate as much as 10 percent of their gross national product from agriculture. Converted farmlands in the river's floodplains have impacted the wetland's ability to hold floodwaters, and floods in 1997 and 2002 caused extensive damage to crops and property. Recent conversions to vegetable and fish farms in the delta also have brought pollution problems. Salt water from the delta has leached into irrigation wells, and this salt has accumulated in both farmers' fields and fishing ponds. Plant crops yielded less and fish suffered from a number of ailments, reducing output.

A number of large-scale economic development projects also have dramatically altered the region. For instance, the construction of the Iron Gate Dam, built in 1972 by the Romanian and Yugoslavian governments, created a reservoir in the valley of the Danube River below Belgrade and caused a 100-foot (30-meter) rise in the water level of the river near the dam. Six villages, totaling 17,000 people, had to relocate their settlements. In addition, the natural spawning and migration patterns of several species of sturgeon were impeded, resulting in a substantial reduction in fish populations in the river.

In the 1980s, the Kakhovka hydroelectric plant was built by the Ukrainian government along the river at the country's eastern border and within sight of Romania. It has resulted in a drop in overall water flow and an increase in riverbank and bottom erosion from significant water releases. The plant also has had the effect of dramatically reducing migrating sturgeon populations.

In 1996, the Cernavoda nuclear power plant was completed in Romania along the lower Danube. It is able to generate 705 megawatts of electricity, or roughly 17 percent of Romania's electricity. A shutdown occurred at the plant in 2009 when a crack was discovered in a water pipe, lasting several weeks. Nuclearelectrica, the state company that runs the facility, stated that no leaks of radioactive material occurred.

Mitigation and Management

Various governments have taken steps to preserve the delta region. The groundwork was first laid by the Convention on Wetlands (better known as the Ramsar Convention on Wetlands), an intergovernmental treaty signed in

The Sulina Canal is one of three channels in the Danube Delta in Romania but the only one navigable by large boats. The canal was straightened and dredged for this purpose, and it forms an economic link between Danube ports and the Black Sea. (*Dick Durrance II/National Geographic/Getty Images*)

Ramsar, Iran, in 1971 that provides the framework for national action and international cooperation for the conservation and wise use of wetlands and their resources. In 1976, for example, the Soviet government designated 160 square miles (414 square kilometers) of the Danube River Delta as a protected Ramsar wetland. That area is now overseen by Romania.

In 1991, the United Nations Educational Scientific and Cultural Organization (UNESCO)—a specialized agency of the United Nations that promotes international cooperation and peace through education, science, and culture— approved the Danube River Delta as a world heritage site and a biosphere reserve, enhancing the international recognition of this unique wetland. A Danube Delta Biosphere Reserve Authority was formed to educate the public about the delta and protect the area. That same year, the Romanian government acted to ban projects that damaged the wetlands, although exemptions were permitted for flood protection projects and maintenance of existing canals. Several delta projects that would have harmed the delta, which were in the planning or construction stage, were halted, including construction of an airport, several factories, a tourism center for several hotels, and seven roads.

Also in 1991, the Ukrainian government designated 2,498 square miles (6,470 square kilometers) of the delta as a Ramsar Site of International Importance. This international recognition for Europe's largest continuous marshland elevated the protection efforts from both the government and private sector.

In an attempt to improve the water quality of the Danube, the International Commission for the Protection of the Danube River (ICPDR) was formed in 1998. The commission is made up of fourteen countries—including Austria, Bosnia and Herzegovina, Bulgaria, Croatia, Czech Republic, Germany, Hungary, Moldavia, Montenegro, Romania, Slovakia, Slovenia, Serbia, and Ukraine—as well as the European Union, which have committed to implementing the Danube River Protection Convention. The treaty, which was signed in 1994 in Sofia, Bulgaria, and came into force in 1998, aims to ensure that surface waters and groundwater within the Danube River Basin are managed and used in a sustainable and equitable manner. The ICPDR's goals include reducing water pollution, overseeing flood control projects, and implementing standards for chemical emissions into the waterway.

The ICPDR set up biological and chemical measuring stations at seventy-nine sites in 2001. A water impact assessment rated the river as "moderately polluted to critically polluted," depending on the location and the time of year. The major cause of biological pollution was determined to be insufficiently treated urban wastewater, due to a lack of updated treatment plants. A recommendation to improve water quality by investing in better technology to remove nutrients at wastewater treatment facilities was a major part of ICPDR's Danube River Basin Management Plan, which was completed in 2009.

In 2003, the Ukrainian government proposed modifications to a waterway in the delta in order to increase shipping traffic up the Danube River from the Black Sea. In the planning stage, the Ukrainian government held discussions with the Romanian government, the United Nations, the European Union, and Ramsar. Dredging and excavating such a deepwater channel through sections of marshland, they found, would eliminate wetland habitats, harm fish and wildlife, and increase suspended sediments and pollution. Although requested by the international agencies to perform an environmental impact study before the project began, the Ukrainian government commenced the project in 2004. After intense negotiations, Ukraine agreed to halt work and complete a thorough impact review before proceeding.

In 2006, a conference on the conservation and sustainable development of the Danube River Delta was held in Odessa, Ukraine. The event included government officials from Moldavia, Romania, and Ukraine and representatives from the European Commission, ICPDR, Ramsar, the United Nations, the World Wildlife Fund, Wetlands International, and other nongovernmental organizations. The participants agreed that cooperative environmental protection efforts must be enhanced. Priorities identified include a stronger political commitment to wetlands, adherence to conservation laws and regulations, sharing scientific information, and better monitoring of wetland conditions. The summary report outlined a number of steps to be taken, including developing a master plan for the management of the delta, expanding the biosphere created by UNESCO in 1991 to include the entire delta, and increasing funding to pay for water quality improvements, educational programs, and the enforcement of wetland protection regulations.

One of the biggest hurdles to improving water quality in the Danube River and its delta wetlands is reconciling long-term regional issues. With 81 million people living in ten countries directly bordering the riverbanks, numerous differences in topography, sociology, and economics exist. In order to achieve results, water quality improvements may need to be tied directly to each country's infrastructure, and the costs of treatment plants may have to be shared among neighboring countries.

Selected Web Sites

Danube Delta National Institute for Research and Development: http://www.indd.tim.ro.

International Commission for the Protection of the Danube River: http://www.icpdr.org.

The Ramsar Convention on Wetlands: http://www.ramsar.org.

Romanian Government Danube Reserve Agency: http://www.ddbra.ro/en.

United Nations World Heritage Site: http://whc.unesco.org.

Further Reading

Gastescu, Petre. *Danube Delta: A Biosphere Reserve*. Constanta, Romania: Dobrogea Editing House, 2006.

Hanganu, J. *Vegetation of the Danube Delta Biosphere Reserve*. Bucharest, Romania: Danube Delta National Institute, 2002.

Jansjy, Libor. *The Danube: Environmental Monitoring of An International River*. New York: United Nations University Press, 2004.

Moore, Peter. *Wetlands*. New York: Facts on File, 2001.

United Nations Educational, Scientific, and Cultural Organization. *Summary from the International Conference on the Conservation and Sustainable Development of the Danube Delta*. Odessa, Ukraine, 2006.

Update on Recent Developments in the Danube Delta. Gland, Switzerland: Ramsar Convention on Wetlands, 2005.

5 The Everglades Florida

Located in the southern portion of Florida, the Everglades is one of the world's largest wetland areas. It originates in the city of Orlando, where the Kissimmee River drains into Lake Okeechobee, the second-largest freshwater lake lying completely within the United States. Occupying nearly 4,000 square miles (10,360 square kilometers), the Everglades spans 40 miles (64 kilometers) east to west and 100 miles (161 kilometers) north to south and drains into the Gulf of Mexico at its southern terminus.

The Everglades is a subtropical biome dominated by sawgrass (*Cladium jamaicense*) prairies and other wide-spanning freshwater wetlands. The ecosystem encompasses a number of varied wetland types, including marshes, bogs, mangroves, riverine forests, and hammocks in the open water.

Nearly 89 percent of the water enters this ecosystem via rain. The water travels across almost level terrain, moving slowly southward; it takes eight months for a droplet to travel the length of the Everglades. At its highest point, this wetland is just 10 feet (3 meters) above sea level.

The Everglades is defined by its surrounding geology. Three hundred thousand years ago, Florida was submerged in the Atlantic Ocean. During and after recent ice ages, the Florida Peninsula was subjected to intense changes. When great quantities of ice melted, the sea level rose to inundate almost the entire state. A deeper ocean also forced the ocean bedrock downward from its weight.

During the submerged times, the decay of sea life resulted in large depositions of calcium carbonate, which combined with sand and rock to form a hard

EVERGLADES WETLAND HABITAT TYPES

Terrestrial Communities
Pineland forests
Hardwood hammocks
Bayheads
Sawgrass prairies
Mangrove and cyprus swamps

Aquatic Communities
Freshwater rivers (including ponds, floodplains, and savannas)
Freshwater brackish marshes
Coastal marshes (including sea grass beds, mangroves, and estuaries)

surface called oolite. This oolitic limestone holds in the water that allowed the Everglades to form.

The vegetation in southern Florida has adapted to the intense heat and violent storms of the drier summer months and the cooler, wetter periods of winter. The region receives up to 55 inches (140 centimeters) of rain per year. It hosts 1,600 types of vascular plants (up to 70 percent are tropical in origin) and 120 species of trees. Among the distinctive and rare plant species in the Everglades is the orchid family, with twenty-five varieties. In mangrove forests, red mangrove (*Rhizophora mangle*), black mangrove (*Avicennia nitida*), and white mangrove (*Laguncularia racemosa*) show their impressive root systems, arching high out of the water with spider-like legs. Regional grasses include muhley grass (*Muhlenbergia filipes*) and cordgrass (*Spartina sp.*).

Abundant Everglades wildlife includes more than 800 species of land and water vertebrates. There are also twenty-five types of mammals classified as threatened or endangered species. These include the elusive Florida panther (*Felis concolor coryi*), on the verge of extinction with less than 100 animals remaining in the state, and the Florida manatee (*Trichechus manatus latirostris*), which had a population of approximately 3,807 in 2009. There are more than 400 bird species, including the wood stork (*Mycteria americana*) and the Florida sand hill crane (*Grus canadensis pratensis*), two tall waterbirds that stalk the shallow pools for fish and shrimp.

Wood storks *(Mycteria americana)* are the only storks that breed in North America; endangered populations remain in North and South Carolina, Georgia, and Florida. Standing up to 4 feet (1.22 meters) high and having wingspans as wide as 5.5 feet (1.7 meters), these birds live in marshes, swamps, and mangroves, feeding on fish, frogs, crayfish, and large insects. Listed as an endangered species since 1984, these stork populations have been impacted due to development resulting in wetland losses and pollution. *(© Nicolas Larento/Fotolia)*

Scientists have cataloged up to sixty species of reptiles and amphibians, including the American alligator (*Alligator mississippiensis*) and the American crocodile (*Crocodylus acutus*). Both troll the waters for larger prey, such as fish, birds, and, upon occasion, deer and other mammals. More than 275 species of fish have been identified; most have adapted to the mix of salt water and freshwater and to living in warm and shallow waters.

Human Uses

Humans first lived near the Everglades 15,000 years ago. Two separate native peoples—the Tequesta on the east and the Calusa on the west—were divided by marshes. These tribes relied on a diet of small game, fish, shellfish, and native vegetation. When the Spanish explorers first arrived in Florida in 1513, the indigenous population exceeded 20,000.

By 1819, when Spain ceded Florida to the United States, however, both tribes had nearly been eliminated through diseases such as chicken pox and smallpox, capture by colonists or members of other tribes, and outright warfare.

Today, about 2,000 Seminole Indians live across southern Florida. Near the Everglades, less than 200 live on the 81-square-mile (210-square-kilometer) Big Cypress Reservation, just south of Lake Okeechobee.

The first government programs to drain the Everglades began soon after Florida became a state in 1845. Efforts were targeted at removing water from the Kissimmee River and basin (located north of the Everglades) to irrigate sugarcane crops. Fifty thousand acres (20,234 hectares) of wetlands were converted to new farmland before 1900.

When floodplains were cleared and wetlands filled in the 1950s, the land was used to graze livestock (mainly cows). By 1960, however, farmers realized that the cows were deficient in several key nutrients from their Everglades wetland plant diet, and such use of sawgrass areas became less common. By 1990, up to 1,040 square miles (2,694 square kilometers) of habitat had been converted to farmlands, and an extensive network of 800 miles (1,287 kilometers) of ditches had been dug for irrigating crops. Agriculture still is a dominant industry in southern Florida, accounting for several billion dollars per year in revenue from various crops, including citrus (mostly oranges and grapefruits), sugarcane, and the raising of livestock.

Public drinking water diversion canals were begun in 1909, and four were completed by 1917, all to take freshwater to the southeastern part of the state. Today, the Everglades's freshwater is the sole source of drinking water for nearly 6 million people in Florida, including residents of Miami-Dade, Monroe, and Palm Beach counties. This use of freshwater is led by the city of Miami, which reported a population of 413,201 in 2008.

The urbanization of southern Florida that began in the mid-twentieth century has resulted in an increased level of residential and business development. A population that has grown from under 500,000 in 1945 to more than 6 million in 2009 has significantly impacted land use in the region, resulting in the development of extensive impervious surfaces, such as roads, parking lots, and buildings. These man-made constructions have contributed to a decline in water quality and an impact on wetlands by limiting natural water infiltration into the soil, by elevating local temperatures through solar heating, and, when precipitation arrives, by releasing a range of pollutants such as animal waste, vehicular oils and coolants, road salt, and garbage.

In addition, warm weather in southern Florida is a big draw for vacationers, especially in the winter months. Tourism accounted for more than 1.4 million visits to the Everglades region in 2007, and it is a vital component of the local economy. Recreational use by local residents also has grown along with the population. Private businesses and the U.S. National Park Service offer visitor centers, trails, water access, and camping areas within the Everglades. Popular activities include hiking, bird watching, wilderness exploration, fishing, kayaking, and other kinds of boating.

Pollution and Damage

After four hurricanes between 1926 and 1948 devastated the state and collectively killed several thousand people, efforts were undertaken to control Lake Okeechobee's floods. The South Florida Water Management District and the U.S. Army Corps of Engineers started the Central and South Florida Project in 1948. Under this project, dozens of levees, dams, hurricane gates, dikes, pumps, ditches, and other structures were installed to limit local flooding. Up to 800 miles (1,287 kilometers) of levees and 500 miles (805 kilometers) of canals were built.

As flood control efforts and drinking water withdrawals occurred, the government drained vast wetland areas. An inventory of the Everglades's wetland losses in the 1970s led scientists to proclaim that the Everglades was dying. By 2005, the area had lost up to 50 percent of its original freshwater wetlands, or the equivalent of nearly 2,000 square miles (5,180 square kilometers) or 1.2 million acres (0.5 million hectares). As a result, there has been a 90 percent population decline of the wading waterbirds that previously inhabited the Everglades—such as cranes, ibises, and herons.

Florida's rapid human population growth continued into the first decade of the twenty-first century, with a count of 18.3 million residents in 2008, compared to 9.7 million in 1980. The growth rate is 900 new Floridians per day, or 328,500 per year.

Population growth also has resulted in a number of biotic impacts. The fish and animal population has become contaminated by mercury from industrial

STATE OF FLORIDA POPULATION GROWTH

Year	Population
1830	34,730
1860	140,424
1900	528,542
1930	1,468,211
1960	4,951,560
1990	12,937,926
2000	15,982,378
2005	17,789,864
2008	18,328,000

Source: U.S. Census Bureau, www.census.gov.

activities; seawater has intruded into freshwater aquifers from excessive human groundwater removals; and added nutrients from nitrogen and phosphorus farm runoff and septic system discharges have caused eutrophication of open waters, turning much of the Everglades into an oxygen-starved "algae pea soup."

Another problem is the number of exotic species introduced into the Everglades, many of which are invasive and have caused considerable pressure on native species. Up to 221 species of plants have been added to the region in the last 200 years. For example, the Brazilian pepper tree (*Schinus terebinthifolius*) and the cajeput tree (*Melaleuca quinquenervia*), with their powerful roots and broad canopies that block out sunshine, have thrived, growing quickly and crowding out native plants.

Mitigation and Management

In 1947, author Marjory Stoneman Douglas's groundbreaking book *The Everglades: River of Grass* alerted the general public to a number of threats to the health of the Everglades's ecosystem:

> There are no other Everglades in the world.
>
> They are, they have always been, one of the unique regions of the earth, remote, never wholly known. Nothing anywhere else is like them: their vast glittering openness, wider than the enormous visible round of the horizon, the racing free saltness and sweetness of their massive winds, under the dazzling blue heights of space. They are unique also in the simplicity, the diversity, the related harmony of the forms of life they enclose. The miracle of the light pours over the green and brown expanse of sawgrass and of water, shining and slow moving below, the grass and water that is the meaning and the central fact of the Everglades of Florida. It is a river of grass.

Later that year, in response to public concern over unrestrained development, the U.S. federal government created the Everglades National Park in the southern portion of the water basin, encompassing 460,000 acres (186,155 hectares). By 1950, the park had grown to 1.2 million acres (500,000 hectares), and by 1999, it had been expanded to 1.5 million acres (600,000 hectares).

In 1969, Douglas established the environmental advocacy organization Friends of the Everglades to protect, restore, and preserve the ecosystem. Shortly thereafter, the organization fought against the construction of a new airport at the edge of the Everglades. After an extensive fight, the airport project was stopped in 1974. A grassroots organization, Friends of the

Everglades has about 4,000 members and continues to serve as a watchdog to the goings on both within the wetlands and the legislative and regulatory circles of Florida.

In 1976, the United Nations Educational, Scientific, and Cultural Organization (UNESCO) designated the Everglades a Biosphere Reserve. This designation was approved because of the region's biodiversity and the pressure of ongoing development that would create further wetland losses and increase water pollution. In 1979, UNESCO added the Everglades to its World Heritage List. And in 1987, the Everglades was designated a Ramsar Site of International Importance.

Unsatisfied with local efforts to prevent wetland damages and losses in the Everglades, the U.S. federal government filed a lawsuit against the South Florida Water Management District in 1989. The suit claimed that the district had allowed a pattern of water degradation and not sufficiently protected the wetlands resources areas. The case was settled in 1991, and the Comprehensive Everglades Restoration Plan (CERP), a thirty-year cleanup program, was implemented in 2000. CERP provides a framework and guide to restore, protect, and preserve the water resources of central and southern Florida, including the Everglades. It covers sixteen counties over an 18,000-square-mile (46,620-square-kilometer) area.

In 1994, the Florida legislature enacted the Florida Everglades Forever Act to implement additional wetland restoration programs. The law increased the natural water flowing through the Everglades by reducing freshwater removals by 28 percent. Another requirement is that urban storm water runoff (from streets, parking lots, and rooftops) must be captured and treated before it is released back into wetland areas.

As a result of this legislation, the farming community also made a number of major improvements. Between 1994 and 2001, the agricultural industry contributed $232 million to cleanup efforts. Up to 40,000 acres (16,187 hectares) of artificial marshes were built to clean up farm water runoff, cutting the phosphorus that was running into the Everglades by 73 percent.

Thanks to these and other efforts, by 2002 scientists and conservationists estimated that 70,000 acres (28,328 hectares) of wetlands had been "brought back" to life in Everglades National Park. Despite such progress in protecting wider areas of wetlands and programs implemented to restore damaged portions, however, the future of the Everglades remains uncertain.

Florida's population surpassed 18 million in 2006. By 2030, it is estimated to reach 27 million. Each new resident requires up to 222 gallons (840 liters) of freshwater per day. This problem is multiplied by the fact that Florida drew 85.8 million visitors in 2006, and that number also is expected to increase.

One solution to the drinking water problem may be desalination plants, which are able to turn salt water from the ocean into freshwater. While these plants are very costly to install and operate, they have been successfully used in some Florida communities, such as Tampa Bay and St. Petersburg.

An additional emergent threat to the Everglades is climate change. As global temperatures have increased, ocean levels have risen up to 3 inches (8 centimeters) in the last 200 years. Evidence of this change has been documented in wetland losses at the southern terminus of the Everglades, where its waterways meet the Gulf of Mexico.

Selected Web Sites

Everglades National Park Site: http://www.nps.gov/ever/.
Friends of the Everglades: http://www.everglades.org.
South Florida Water Management District: http://www.sfwmd.gov.
State of Florida Everglades Forever Site: http://www.dep.state.fl.us/everglades forever/.
University of Miami School of Law, Everglades Forever Act: http://www.law. miami.edu/library/everglades/statutes/state/florida/E_forever.htm.

Further Reading

Carter, W. Hodding. *Stolen Water: Saving the Everglades from Its Friends, Foes, and Florida.* New York: Atria, 2004.
Douglas, Marjory Stoneman. *The Everglades: River of Grass.* 1947. Sarasota, FL: Pineapple, 2007.
Grunwald, Michael. *The Swamp: The Everglades, Florida, and Politics of Paradise.* New York: Simon and Schuster, 2006.
Marx, Trish. *Everglades Forever: Restoring America's Great Wetland.* New York: Lee and Low, 2004.
Petuch, Edward. *The Geology of the Everglades and Adjacent Areas.* Boca Raton, FL: CRC, 2007.
United Nations Environment Programme. *Everglades National Park, Florida, USA.* Cambridge, UK: World Conservation Monitoring Centre, 2003.

6 | The Pantanal
Brazil, Bolivia, and Paraguay

Landlocked in the heart of South America sits an immense low-altitude alluvial plain called the Pantanal. Rather than a single wetland area, the Pantanal is an expansive patchwork of habitats, featuring dozens of freshwater marshes, bogs, swamps, rivers, and lakes.

Located within the northern Paraguay River Basin, this massive wetland complex exists in three separate countries, with 80 percent in central Brazil, 15 percent in eastern Bolivia, and 5 percent in northeastern Paraguay. At over 81,000 square miles (209,790 square kilometers) in size, the Pantanal is one of the planet's largest wetland areas, stretching along 1,584 miles (2,549 kilometers) of the Paraguay River from northern Brazil to Argentina.

Brazil's Pantanal occupies an area that is 53,352 square miles (138,182 square kilometers) in size and takes up nearly 40 percent of the entire watershed. It is seventeen times larger than the Florida Everglades and comprises nearly 3 percent of the world's wetlands.

The lowlands within the Pantanal are either permanently or seasonally saturated with water, based upon their elevation. This temperate region receives up to 64 inches (163 centimeters) of rain per year in the highest elevations and half that amount in the drier lowlands. The wet season runs from October to March, and the dry season is April to September. Once the rains have slowed in the spring, up to 80 percent of the Pantanal is submerged. Up to a third of these wetlands dry up through the summer months. Temperatures range from 32 to 100 degrees Fahrenheit (0 to 38 degrees Celsius).

The word *Pantanal* translates into "the big swamp" in Portuguese. This wetland's origins can be found in its distant geologic history. Underlying the terrain is a bottom layer of metamorphic rocks, consisting of mostly granitoids (very hard igneous rock formations), formed during the Archean Period, 2.5 billion years ago. Thick deposits of sedimentary rock settled on top of this bottom layer during the Ordovician-Silurian Period, 443 million years ago.

The Pantanal basin features gradually sloping sides. The soils in the area are dense, due to their high clay content, and drain poorly when saturated. In addition, the multiple rivers that drain the water from this basin have only one narrow exit—the Paraguay River. With only this one outlet, regular flooding has influenced the formation of wetlands in the region.

What makes the Pantanal special is the wide range of vegetation and wildlife that thrives here. More than 1,863 animals and 1,537 plants have been identified in this humid temperate zone.

Vegetation has adapted to the large floods of the spring and grows rapidly once the waters surge to form rivers, marshes, lakes, and lagoons. The amount of water that remains in a particular area determines the range of vegetation— from palm-type trees and woody plants in moist spots on the edge of standing water to dozens of types of shrubs and more than 100 species of grasses and sedges where there is standing water year-round.

Some of the Pantanal's unique vegetation includes species of floating plants that fill the shallow lakes and oxbows. These include the water hyacinth (*Eichhornia crassipes*) and water lettuce (*Pistia stratiotes*), both of which extend their roots into the water to absorb nutrients. Rooted wetland vegetation such as cattails (*Typha dominguensis*) and the soft-stemmed bulrush (*Scirpus validus*) provides an exceptional habitat for many species of birds.

The wildlife that lives within the wetland basin includes up to ninety-five species of mammals, forty-six of which are threatened or endangered, such as the jaguar (*Panthera onca*) and the maned wolf (*Chrysocyon brachyurus*). There are 162 species of reptiles, including up to 10 million alligator-like caimans (*Caiman crocodilus),* at an approximate density of one every 2.8 square miles (7.3 square kilometers), and forty species of amphibians.

The year-round bird diversity within the broader region of the Pantanal has been estimated at an impressive 656 species, belonging to sixty-six separate families. This number includes a range of large birds, including the world's largest stork, the jabiru (*Jabiru mycteria*), which is 6 feet (1.8 meters) tall. The threatened American rhea (*Rhea americana*), a species similar to the ostrich, is the largest American bird species. Loss of habitat from development and over-hunting have led to efforts to protect these flightless birds.

More than a dozen native parrot species live in the Pantanal, including the green-winged macaw (*Ara chloroptera*) and the largest parrot on the planet, the

Piranhas are native to South America, though some have been discovered as far away as the United States and England. These fish are characterized by their razor-sharp teeth; sometimes, hungry schools of them will feed in a frenzy. (© Christopher Howey/Fotolia)

endangered hyacinth macaw (*Anodorhynchus hyacinthinus*). A captured hyacinth macaw can fetch more than $10,000 on the black market for sale as a pet. Hunted as food and for their vivid feathers, only 5,000 remain on Earth, and the majority live in remote portions of the Pantanal.

Up to 263 species of freshwater fish have been documented in the Patanal—including dorado (*Salminus maxillosus*), pintado (*Pseudoplatystoma corruscans*), and piranha (*Pygocentrus nattereri*). These freshwater fish living in the Pantanal must cope with difficult living conditions. There are large fluctuations in water levels from the rainy season to the drier season. The water often is very low in oxygen, due to its slow drainage. And water flows often are sediment-free, primarily due to the low drainage angle.

Human Uses

Residents of the Pantanal hold considerable respect for its biodiversity. A common statement, "*O Pantanal é vida,*" which translates as "The Pantanal is life," emphasizes the people's admiration for the land.

One factor influencing the health of the Pantanal ecosystem is the low resident human population. Those living in the region number around 206,000, or about one person per 395 acres (160 hectares), according to 2007 estimates. This low population has resulted in little development and infrastructure, such as roads, airports, rail lines, and boats. The economy is resource driven, and local commerce focuses on forestry, mining, fishing, farming (crops and cattle), and tourism.

Ecotourism, tourism based on highlighting the beauty and value of particular ecosystems, is a common draw to the Pantanal. However, due to the lack of local airports with jet service, limited accommodations, few good roads, and insufficient support from local government, this tourism segment has struggled to grow, especially in more remote areas.

Nevertheless, Brazil's private industry offers a mixture of environment-based tours, featuring specific destinations such as a waterfall or a particular wildlife habitat. Visitors can choose from a variety of multi-day packages that include lodging, food, and daily excursions. Some adventure packages focus on wildlife observation and conservation, and some feature such activities as horseback riding, hunting, and fishing.

Pollution and Damage

One of the direct threats to wetland species comes from outside markets that crave South American exports. Illegal poaching, especially by poorer residents who are paid well for accessing remote habitats, has been a persistent issue. Black market animal removals peaked in the 1980s when up to 1 million caiman skins were collected per year. Hunters, private collectors, and zoos have trapped and removed the deep woods jaguar (*Panthera onca*), contributing to the decimation of this animal population and its placement on endangered species lists.

The Spix's macaw (*Cyanopsitta spixii*) was driven to near extinction in 1988; preservationists' hope for regrowth of the species comes from captive populations in the United States and Western Europe. Other birds, such as the hyacinth macaw, face a similar fate as the demand for large domestic parrots increases.

In northern Brazil, the Manso River feeds into the Cuiabá River, which drains into the Pantanal basin. In 1999, a 300-foot-high (91.4-meter-high) dam was built on the Manso River with a 200-megawatt hydroelectric power-generating facility. Behind the Manso Dam is a 98,842-acre (40,000-hectare) reservoir. The dam holds back 60 percent of the water that previously flowed to the Cuiabá River, causing damage to wetlands and wildlife, altering native fish spawning routes, and submerging 154 square miles (399 square kilometers) previously used by animals and humans.

The Hidrovia Project, which has been supported by the governments of Argentina and Paraguay since the 1990s, aims to enable large ocean vessels to travel 2,000 miles (3,218 kilometers) up the Paraguay River from the Atlantic Ocean. The project proposes massive river dredging and widening, as well as the construction of ports where up to 1,000-foot-long (305-meter-long) boats can dock and turn around. Although initially planned as a measure for tourism boats, the project would support a broader range of economic development. The extended waterway would create an outlet to the sea for landlocked Paraguay and Bolivia and an international port for Uruguay, increase export possibilities for Argentina, and potentially provide a financial boost to Brazil's poor western region. As of 2009, however, Brazilian government officials had not approved their country's segment of the project, noting that most of the boats that would take advantage of the changes would be international cruise lines, not Brazilian boat lines, and that irreparable harm would be caused to the wetlands and wildlife of the Pantanal.

The Pantanal boasts two centuries of ranching history, which includes significant impacts to wetlands. Cowboys of this region, known as *Pantaneiros* or "bog trotters," work on at least 260 ranches. By the turn of the twentieth

Cattle ranching is a dominant economic activity in the Brazilian Pantanal, with most ranches passed down from one generation to the next. Many of the horses used by the ranchers have adapted to the wet terrain by developing strong lungs that aid them in eating submerged grass and hardened hoofs that resist rot from water immersion. *(Laurie Noble/Getty Images)*

THREATS TO THE PANTANAL WETLANDS

Threat	Location	Cause
Increased sediments	Taquari and São Lourenço rivers	Increased farming, forestry, road building.
Dam construction	Several waterways	Small dams used for irrigation, larger dams for electricity.
Water pollution	City of Cuiabá, State of Mato Grosso	Urban discharge, gold mining, farm pesticide runoff.
Fishing without licenses	Regionwide	No government over sight in Brazil, Bolivia, or Paraguay.
Large developments	City of Corumbá, Paraguay River	Gas pipelines, river modifications.

Source: Brazilian Upper Paraguay River Conservation Plan, 2005.

century, ranchers had converted more than 988,000 acres (399,829 hectares) of forests, grasslands, and wetlands into cattle ranges to support 2.5 million cattle. Seventy years later, the majority of private ranches held a total of 5 million animals on properties up to 24,000 acres (9,713 hectares) in size.

Soy farming in the region north of the Pantanal also poses risks to the wetlands. As global diets have called for abundant sources of protein, soybean farming in the region has increased. Farms that were formed in floodplains in the 1990s have resulted in an increase in toxic runoff pollution—silt, fertilizers, pesticides, and human waste—that has concentrated in the Pantanal. In addition, isolated soybean farmers are seeking government assistance to reduce river travel times by dredging and straightening waterways.

The government of Brazil documented these and other threats to the Pantanal in its Upper Paraguay River Conservation Plan. In 2005, this $16 million effort studied the five major factors that are degrading the biotic health of the region and provided a number of recommendations for better managing the region's natural resources.

Mitigation and Management

Despite the fact that nearly 80 percent of the Pantanal is privately owned, a movement is under way to conserve broad swaths of Brazil's wetland resource area. This includes an increase in government ownership of land to enhance its protection. As of 2000, the Brazilian government had set aside 80 percent of the country's public lands. Bolivia, which holds less than 10 percent of the Pantanal wetlands, has protected its biodiverse regions by conserving 90 percent of its public tracts.

The pace of land protection efforts is juxtaposed with a variety of large-scale proposals to improve the local economy. These economic projects have the potential for considerable negative impacts on the wetlands by creating pollution, altering water movements, reducing flood control, and otherwise degrading wetland habitats. For example, a proposed $300 million Atlantic-Pacific Corridor would feature roads from Bolivia to Brazil across the Pantanal. Two separate routes would allow for truck transport of produce and goods, as well as support expanded tourism. A second, $4 billion project would connect two Pantanal rivers, the Paraguay and the Paraná, with a 2,138-mile-long (3,440-kilometer-long) deepwater channel.

The formation of government parks has allowed the public to access a variety of Pantanal regions. The Brazilian government created the Pantanal Matogrossense National Park in 1981 in the northeast, a 520-square-mile (1,347-square-kilometer) preserve in the state of Mato Grosso. The area was designated a Ramsar Site of International Importance in 1993. Featuring wetland areas called *cerrados* (savannas), this park's large wet meadows of grassy plants thrive in the flooded conditions.

In 1997, the Bolivian federal government designated the Otuquis National Park. Located in western Bolivia in one of the most remote areas of the Pantanal, the national park is 3,883 square miles (10,057 square kilometers) in size and features wetlands in 44 percent of its area. The San Matías Natural Area of Integrated Management features 11,268 square miles (29,184 square kilometers) of protected open space.

In 1998, the World Wildlife Fund, the world's largest multinational conservation organization, and the Noel Kempff Mercado Museum of Natural History in Bolivia led a series of planning workshops that discussed methods for improving and caring for protected areas of the Pantanal. Workshop participants created a series of short-, medium-, and long-term goals and formed a steering committee made up of representatives from environmental groups, cultural groups, and the governments of Bolivia, Brazil, and Paraguay.

That same year, the Pantanal Private Natural Heritage Reserve, a private park dedicated to the preservation of its biotic inhabitants, was formed near the Pantanal Matogrossense National Park. This 339-square-mile (878-square-kilometer) parcel, called Poconé Pantanal, is the largest private park in South America. It contains a diversity of wetlands and was designated a Ramsar Site of International Importance in 2002. The park hosts South America's largest nesting area of the wood stork (*Mycteria americana*), which hunts for many of the 260 fish species that live in the area.

Selected Web Sites

The Brazilian Cacti Project, Geology of Brazil: http://www.brcactaceae.org/geology.html.

National Geographic Pantanal Profile: http://www.nationalgeographic.com/wildworld/profiles/terrestrial/nt/nt0907.html.

United Nations World Heritage Site: http://whc.unesco.org.

World Wildlife Fund: http://www.worldwildlife.org.

Further Reading

Fraser, Lauchlan, and Paul A. Keddy, eds. *The World's Largest Wetlands: Ecology and Conservation.* Cambridge, UK: Cambridge University Press, 2005.

Mittermeier, Russell. *Pantanal: South America's Wetland Jewel.* Arlington, VA: Conservation International, 2005.

Ramsar Convention on Wetlands. *Site Summary: Reserva Particular do Patrimonio Natural SESC Pantanal.* Gland, Switzerland: Ramsar Convention, 2003.

Swarts, Frederick. *The Pantanal in the 21st Century.* New York: Hudson MacArthur, 2000.

7 Lake Poyang China

Lake Poyang, China's largest freshwater body, sits in the southeastern part of the country, in northern Jiangxi Province. Measuring 105 miles (169 kilometers) west to east by 10 miles (16 kilometers) north to south, the lake features 1,208 square miles (3,129 square kilometers) of freshwater wetlands, including marshes, bogs, floodplains, and forested swamplands.

Although locals call Lake Poyang "the mother lake" for its abundant wetlands and bird life, the area is also intensely fished, farmed, and mined to support a regional population of approximately 10 million people. The climate in this region is subtropical with 71 inches (180 centimeters) of rain per year.

The depression in which Lake Poyang exists was formed millions of years ago through tectonic and volcanic activity. Over several hundred thousand years, mountain valleys were shaped by erosion and glacial action. The lake itself, however, is very young. It came into existence 1,600 years ago, around 400 B.C.E. At that time, the main branch of the Yangtze River jumped its track from its northern flow to a southerly direction. The new course blocked the drainage of several other area rivers. In less than a month, those pooled to form Lake Poyang, named after the nearby Poyang Mountain.

The lake features a unique flooding cycle. During the peak of the spring rains, Lake Poyang is fed by two rivers—the Gan and the Xiu—and back flowed by the flooding Yangtze River. The hydrology of this body of water plays a central role in the life cycle of adjacent wetlands.

With an average springtime depth of 24 feet (7 meters), during flood stage the lake expands to almost 2,000 square miles (5,180 square kilometers) of open water and reaches into nearby floodplains. Over the summer months, the water level gradually decreases, reaching a diminished size of 386 square miles (1,000 square kilometers) by the winter, just 20 percent of its size in the spring. By late summer, 30 vertical feet (9 meters) of water has flowed downstream on the Gan, Xiu, and Yangtze rivers. The largest freshwater body in China is transformed into nine separate lakes.

As water levels drop, an impressive diversity of up to 600 species of wetland plants emerge from the muddy soils. More than 102 aquatic vascular plant species, including eelgrass (*Vallisneria spiralis*) and pondweed (*Potamogeton distinctus*), thrive in the warm, shallow waters. Better-drained marshes contain grasses from the *Graminae* family and several sedges from the *Cyperaceae* family. Fish feed on the 154 families of phytoplankton that grow in the lake. In all, dense vegetation in the Lake Poyang basin covers an 873-square-mile (2,261-square-kilometer) area.

These wetlands provide an ideal habitat for 332 species of birds that make up a population of 100,000 during the summer months and crest at 500,000 during seasonal migrations. Up to 95 percent of the world's Siberian cranes (*Grus leucogeranus*) spend their winters in the Lake Poyang wetlands. Almost the entire world population of the white-naped crane (*Grus vipio*) lives in this basin, numbering nearly 4,000.

The wetland areas are rich in diversity of other wildlife, including eighty-seven species of reptiles, sixty species of amphibians, and eighty-four species

BIRDS OF POYANG

Common Name	Scientific Name	Characteristics
White-tailed eagle	*Haliaeetus albicilla*	Cousin of American bald eagle. Eats sand eels and nests in private stands of trees, sometimes for generations.
Great bustard	*Otis tarda*	One of the heaviest birds (up to 35 pounds, or 15.88 kilograms), this threatened species lives in wet meadows. When scared, it often runs rather than flies.
Chinese merganser	*Mergus squamatus*	An endangered duck species that dives to feed. Less than 2,500 remain in China.
Imperial eagle	*Aquila heliaca*	Classified as a vulnerable species, these eagles often winter in the Poyang Basin, relying on small mammals for food.
White stork	*Ciconia ciconia*	Exceeding 50 inches (127 centimeters) tall with a wingspan of over 80 inches (203 centimeters), this wetland species lives on large insects, frogs, and rodents.

of mammals. Lake Poyang features 122 species of fish, including silver carp (*Hypophthalmichthys molitrix*), snake-headed fish (*Channa argus*), and whitebait (*Galaxias maculates*).

Human Uses

China has 10 percent of the world's wetlands, and these wetlands cover almost 3 percent of the country. China also holds nearly 25 percent of the global human population. As of 2006, 10 million people lived in Jiangxi Province. Around the lake itself, sixty local towns make up a population of 20,000 residents. These statistics translate into China's economic need to utilize all natural resources on an intensive level, including freshwater and farmland, which has led to considerable pressure on wetlands.

The floodplains of Lake Poyang contain rich soils that are high in nutrients such as nitrogen, phosphorus, and potassium. Once the floodwaters recede in the summer, bright green vegetation grows over mile upon mile of lowlands. In the intense sun and moisture of a subtropical climate, plants grow more than 1 inch (2.5 centimeters) each day, allowing at least two crop plantings and harvests during the warm months.

Since 1998, mud and sand dredging has become a mainstay of economic development on Lake Poyang. Up to half a dozen boats with 1,000-ton capacities use hydraulic pressure to vacuum mud, sand, and silt onto decks where the earth is dewatered and trucked away to be sold as fertile soil. One boat can haul away soil worth up to $13,000 in a single day. Removal of sediment, however, turns the lake bottom, wetlands, and wildlife habitats into wastelands where no vegetative, fish, or clam species can survive. Chinese wetland managers also have stated that the cacophony of dredging noise has caused extensive underwater noise pollution, repelling larger fish, especially those that use sonar to navigate and locate food.

Fishing accounts for the largest segment of the local economy, and nearly 40,000 tons of fish are taken from the lake each year. The most commonly caught fish is Crucian carp (*Carassius carassius*), which grows up to 3 pounds (1.4 kilograms). In winter, some of the nine lakes have their water levels temporarily lowered by up to half by town authorities to make harvesting fish easier. This is performed by blocking channels between the lakes—the upper lakes increase in height, and the lower lakes drain considerably. After the catch is complete, the water levels are restored. Fishermen use open deck boats, longlines, several types of nets, electricity shock fields, and even trained cormorants to haul their catch.

Bird watching is one of the tourist draws in the Lake Poyang area. Ecotourism has emerged as a popular growth industry. One example includes

Shahushan township, which sits on the shores of Poyang Lake. Shahushan has 5,000 residents, 966 of which have relocated to the community since 1998 in a government resettlement program. In order to better leverage the 15 square miles (39 square kilometers) of wetlands and lakefront in the township and grow the local economy, the town accepted a grant in 2001 from the World Wildlife Fund to establish several businesses to operate an ecotourism program. The effort has been a success, drawing visitors from the region and from overseas.

Pollution and Damage

Lake Poyang hosts 1,208 square miles (3,129 square kilometers) of wetland habitats, mostly marshy expanses with dense grasses. Researchers estimate that up to 40 percent of the lake's wetlands have been lost in the last 200 years due to economic development, impacts from population growth, and human-induced hydrology changes.

Large water-level fluctuations in this and other lakes cause harm to their associated wetlands. Since the 1980s, freshwater lakes and wetlands across China have decreased by 4,633 square miles (12,000 square kilometers). In addition, more than 1,500 small lakes along the Yangzte River above Lake Poyang have been converted into farmland or aquaculture areas; this has reduced the ability of adjacent wetlands to hold floodwaters and thus has made Lake Poyang more prone to flooding.

Taking advantage of the richness of the soils along the lake, in the 1950s provincial officials created a program to transform floodplains and wetlands into bountiful farmlands that would require no enrichment for up to five years and produce substantially greater crop yields. Although the program yielded large quantities of vegetables and fruit orchards, it also resulted in several hundred thousand acres of wetlands being drained along the edge of Lake Poyang. In 1986, the effort was halted and wetland reclamation became a government priority.

Since that time, the Chinese government has recognized 217 wetland areas across the country; ninety-five have been protected as nature preserves. And, in the twenty-first century, the rate of wetland loss has slowed.

One casualty of China's economic growth is the region's river dolphin (*Lipotes vexillifer*), also called the *baiji*. Since the late twentieth century, human activities—including dam construction, intensive boating traffic, water pollution, overfishing, and predation—have harmed this freshwater dolphin. The baiji, which numbered around 6,000 in 1950, lived in Lake Poyang and was last seen there in 2004. After three years of no reported sightings and an extensive three-week survey in 2006, scientists reported that the baiji is assumed to be extinct.

One of the problems associated with population growth in the Poyang Lake region is the pollution of the lake's wetlands and freshwater resources. This includes the discharge of untreated human waste and runoff of fertilizers and chemicals from adjacent farms. Unless effective measures are taken to clean up contaminated freshwater in the lake, water quality will continue to decline, threatening both humans and the ecological balance in the waterway. *(Mark Ralston/AFP/Getty Images)*

Learning from the likely loss of the baiji, scientists and conservationists are studying and tracking the finless river porpoise (*Neophocaena phocaeniodes*), known as the *jiangzhu* or "river pig." Approximately 500 jiangzhu live in the lake. A study in 2006 by the Chinese Academy of Sciences found that although nearly 1,400 of these animals exist in China, their population has been shrinking by more than 7 percent per year. Scientists estimate that more than a dozen jiangzhu die each year from getting tangled in nets, swimming into electric fishing fields, or ingesting toxic food or plastic. Some fishermen use guns to shoot jiangzhu to stop the porpoises from encroaching on their catch, further contributing to the endangerment of the species.

Mitigation and Management

Despite insufficient funding and weak regulations, the national and provincial governments have come a long way over the last twenty-five years in protecting the wetlands of Lake Poyang. In 1983, in an effort to safeguard the lake's large population of cranes, the provincial government formed the 55,351-acre (22,400-hectare) Lake Poyang Nature Reserve in a portion of the lake. In 1992, the Chinese government created the Jiangxi Poyang Lake National Reserve, encompassing 55,351 acres (22,400 hectares). That same year, Lake Poyang was nominated and accepted as a Ramsar Site of International Importance.

However, this designation did not include the entire wetland, just the original nature reserve. In order to restore fish populations in Poyang and protect them during the spawning season, the provincial government imposed a strict limit on fishing in 1986 and banned all fishing for a period of three months each spring. The temporary government ban includes both fishing from boats on open water and tackle use from the shore.

Also in 1986, the provincial authorities began a campaign that promoted fish breeding in contained ponds and encouraged fishermen to change jobs to increase fish populations. The initial campaign failed due to limited follow-through, but it was implemented a second time in 2006, with increased government oversight.

In 1996, Ramsar Convention officials visited the region and revealed a number of wetland conservation deficiencies. Convention recommendations to the provincial government included expanding the protected wetland areas; investing in facilities and equipment for the Jiangxi Poyang Lake National Reserve; increasing funding for reserve staff and research; improving provincial enforcement efforts; and expanding educational programs to increase community awareness of and support for the wetlands. In 1998, the provincial government launched a campaign to stabilize the water depth of Lake Poyang, in order to limit flooding and subsequent problems.

By 2004, officials had removed illegal drainage ditches and dams to increase water coverage from 1,505 square miles (3,898 square kilometers) to 1,969 square miles (5,100 square kilometers). This action submerged certain wetlands, resulting in their loss, but it also created favorable conditions for new, larger wetlands to form. In addition, provincial and national leaders increased funding for the region, although long-term investments, such as reserve expansion, have not occurred.

In 2005, the World Wildlife Fund (WWF) embarked on an effort to develop a plan for Integrated River Basin Management in Lake Poyang in coordination with the China Council for International Cooperation on Environment and Development, a high-level advisory body to the national government. The WWF plan contained an environmental and economic analysis of the region and a series of recommendations to better conserve the wetlands. These recommendations included an expansion of ecotourism efforts and rehabilitation of wetland sites.

The Lake Poyang wetlands are difficult to protect in part because of the local approach to management. Many residents perceive wildlife as ecologically important to conserve but also note that natural habitats should be used as a human resource. Wetlands do not exist to be set aside, some residents argue, but rather to be utilized by the local economy.

A Chinese worker shovels dredged silt along the Yangtze River, part of an attempt to keep the entrance to Lake Poyang, China's largest freshwater lake, open and free flowing near the city of Hukou. The silt buildup is a result of several factors, including wetland losses and deforestation in the area. *(Mark Ralston/AFP/Getty Images)*

Modifying an existing industry requires a broad campaign and significant government investment. Local officials have discussed addressing the over-fishing issue by reducing year-round catch limits and increasing no-fishing zones. Silt and mud removals are under regulatory review to lessen their impact on the environment. Finally, limits on farmlands in wetland areas already have resulted in restored wetlands.

Local government leaders have learned that each task must be met with an educational plan, because many conservation measures impose financial burdens on a population for which industries such as fishing, farming, and dredging have been the foundations of its livelihood. An overarching goal, as outlined by the WWF, must be to simultaneously enhance ecological protection and elevate the standard of living for the residents of the Lake Poyang region.

Selected Web Sites

Chinese University Report: http://www.iseis.cuhk.edu.hk/yuenyuen/project/poyang/poyang.htm.

Poyang Lake Ecology Study: http://www.savingcranes.org/poyanglakeproject.html.

Ramsar Convention on Wetlands: http://www.ramsar.org.

Science Museum of China, Lake Museum: http://www.kepu.com.cn/english/lake/.

Further Reading

Chen, S. *Modeling the Impacts of Land Use on Sediment Load in Wetlands of the Poyang Lake Basin.* St. Joseph, MI: American Society of Agricultural and Biological Engineers, 2006.

Chinese University of Hong Kong. *Monitoring the Dynamic Changes of Poyang Lake Wetlands Through Remote Sensing.* Shatin, Hong Kong: Institute of Space and Earth Information Science, 2005.

Datong, Ning. *An Assessment of the Economic Losses Resulting From Various Forms of Environmental Degradation in China.* Beijing: China Environmental Sciences Press, 2001.

Shen, Dajun. *Mountain-River-Lake Integrated Water Resources Development Program.* Beijing: China Institute of Water Resources and Hydropower Research, 2006.

8 Aral Sea
Kazakhstan and Uzbekistan

Estimated to be nearly 5 million years old, the Aral Sea is a large saline lake in Central Asia, located between Kazakhstan and Uzbekistan. It sits in the center of the great deserts of central Asia—the Betpakdala, Karakum, and Kyzyl Kum—and is surrounded by the Turan Plain with mountains on the east and south. The region receives less than 10 inches (25 centimeters) of rain per year, and the area as a whole is subject to high rates of evaporation due to an arid weather pattern and landscape.

In 1960, the Aral Sea was the fourth-largest inland body of water in the world, measuring 26,254 square miles (67,998 square kilometers) in size and spanning 450 miles (724 kilometers) from north to south and 175 miles (282 kilometers) from west to east. Once a thriving natural habitat, by the turn of the twenty-first century environmentalists had ranked this wetland region as one of the worst human-induced ecological disasters to date. Today, as the result of an international effort, parts of the Aral Sea region are being restored to improved health.

Much of the Aral Sea's size and water balance are determined by river inflow and evaporation. Before considerable regional development in the 1960s, this water body was salty, but its salinity was low (averaging less than one-third of the salinity of the ocean), and the sea was inhabited mostly by freshwater species. It contained 1.3 million acres (500,000 hectares) of wetlands, including freshwater marshes, bogs, and swamps. There were 2,600 lakes along the rivers that fed the wetlands. Filled mainly by the Syr Darya and Amu Darya rivers, the Aral Sea received 14 trillion gallons (53 trillion liters) of freshwater per year. There were

INDICATORS IN THE ARAL SEA BASIN

Indicator	Unit	1960	1970	1980	1990	2000
Population	Million people	14.1	20	26.8	33.6	41.5
Irrigated land	Million acres	11.1	12.7	17	18.7	19.7
Water removed	Cubic miles/year	14.5	22.6	28.9	27.8	25.1
Aral Sea inflows	Cubic miles/year	13.4	10.3	4	0.95	0.71

Source: Gulnara Roll, *Aral Sea: Experience and Lessons Learned.* Washington, DC: World Bank, 2006.

at least 319 bird species recorded in the region, and 179 of these nested in the wetlands. The area supported vibrant agricultural and fishing communities.

Massive irrigation projects undertaken by the former Soviet Union beginning in the 1950s and continuing over a forty-year period, however, led to an overall reduction of the Aral Sea's surface area by more than half. As water from the Syr Darya and Amu Darya rivers was redirected to arid lands to grow cotton, rice, and other crops, the Aral Sea shrunk to 150 miles (241 kilometers) from north to south and less than 100 miles (161 kilometers) from west to east.

In a few decades, the entire southern portion of the Aral Sea dried up, and its wetlands, wildlife, and habitats disappeared. Water levels dropped by 40 feet (12 meters), and what inflow did continue was full of toxins, salt, and excessive nutrients such as nitrogen and phosphorus.

By 1989, the Aral Sea had separated into two water bodies, a northern portion called the Small Aral Sea and a southern portion called the Big Aral Sea. The previous year, the Soviet Union had acknowledged the gravity of the environmental damage and had declared the wetlands a "natural disaster area." In 1991, the Soviet Union dissolved, and seven countries in the watershed—Afghanistan, Iran, Kazakhstan, the Kyrgyz Republic (Kyrgyzstan), Tajikistan, Turkmenistan, and Uzbekistan—experienced an unprecedented environmental crisis.

By 2000, environmentalists documented a decline from 168 bird species to thirty-two. Waterfowl such as the white-headed duck (*Oxyura leucocephala*) and the great white pelican (*Pelecanus roseus*) were barely surviving. In 2003, the Aral Sea—still shrinking in size—divided again, into western and eastern sections, leaving four separate bodies of water.

By 2005, the wetlands of the Aral Sea had been decimated. Only 250,000 of the original 1.3 million acres (500,000 hectares) remained, and due to the resultant high salinity (four to eight times the original levels), salt-tolerant vegetation expanded, while varieties not tolerant to salt perished. Many species of wildlife, including birds and fish, died due to these conditions.

Human Uses

More than 26 million people live in the watershed surrounding the Aral Sea, which is spread across five countries and 598,203 square miles (1,549,346 square kilometers). Despite semi-arid conditions, agriculture plays a central role in the economy. Up to 6,000 years ago, small farming communities began to divert water for farming. Initial measures such as gravity-fed, hand-dug canals evolved into a complex system of dikes and a maze of channels and retention ponds.

Scientists estimated that by 1970 up to 1,000 separate man-made irrigation channels were dug to bring water from the river to farmland. These unlined and uncovered irrigation trenches often lost more water through seepage or evaporation than they transported to the cotton fields in southern Russia. In addition, nutrients, defoliants, and pesticides entered the rivers through natural runoff and were carried to the Aral Sea. Nearly 19.5 million acres (7.9 million hectares) of cotton were in production by 1990.

In 1950, fishing in the Aral Sea was the lifeblood for 60,000 Russians; the fish caught exceeded 100 million pounds per year. By 1970, receding waters had left villages previously located on the sea up to 10 miles (16.1 kilometers) from the water's edge. Twenty of the two dozen commercially sought fish species disappeared due to the high salt content of the water. The fishing industry collapsed, and large, rusting boats were left marooned in a new desert.

Despite the loss of many fish species, fishermen still could earn $100 on a good day by hauling in flounder and carp, an above-average wage in this poverty-stricken region. Therefore, small-scale fishing of the remaining salt-tolerant species by local fishermen continued.

Pollution and Damage

Although the communities around the Aral Sea began to feel the ecological impacts on the region in the 1970s, it took several more decades for wide-scale ecological damage to accumulate. As waters receded, the Aral Sea wetlands shrunk.

As the water levels descended, new wetlands formed for short periods; however, by the mid-1990s, nearly 80 percent of the wetlands had been lost. It was not until this time that the international community realized the scope of the loss and began to calculate the fish, amphibian, reptile, mammal, plant, and microbiological extirpations from these wetlands.

In 1948, the Soviet Union established a chemical and biological weapons testing facility on Vozrozhdeniye Island in the middle of the Aral Sea—an area that is part of present-day Kazakhstan and Uzbekistan. Up to 1,000 people lived there between 1960 and 1980, testing typhus, encephalitis, smallpox, and other microbiological strains. This site served as the world's largest burial ground for hundreds of tons of anthrax when the facility closed in 1992.

Although the waste was treated twice with bleach before being buried, according to tests conducted in 2000, deadly bacteria are still alive in the burial pits. And as the Aral Sea continues to shrink, this 77-square-mile (199-square-kilometer) hazardous island eventually will be connected to the mainland. The Russian cleanup that was planned for the early 1990s did not occur; the United

This 2009 satellite image of the Aral Sea shows the 1960 historic coastline (outlined in black) and the current coastline (shown as the sections of open water in the northern portion). *(U.S. National Aeronautics and Space Administration)*

States subsequently was asked to help with the cleanup in 1995 and provided $6 million and technical assistance for this effort.

The environmental, economic, and social impacts from the shrinking Aral Sea have been devastating to local communities. The northern city of Aral, with a population of 35,000, shrank to half its size between 1980 and 2000. It changed from a thriving coastal seaport to a run-down and poverty-stricken inland city located a staggering 50-mile (80-kilometer) drive from the water's edge. Malnutrition and disease became common. Instead of a diet rich in fish, meat, and fresh produce, most families now live on bread, teas, and, rarely, canned foods. Anemia, high infant mortality rates, and suicide emerged in addition to other physical and mental health issues. Seeking work, thousands streamed out of isolated communities and into the Russian oil fields in the late 1990s. Wide swathes of neighborhoods were abandoned.

As the Aral Sea's basin dried up, strong dry winds blew salt and pesticides into the air. Up to 40,000 tons of toxic dust spread across the region each year. Farms located hundreds of miles away from the lake developed high salt content in their soils; in some cases, up to 60 percent of farmland has been contaminated. Local health experts also consider airborne salt and dust as factors contributing to high rates of respiratory illnesses such as asthma and infections, stomach and esophageal cancers, and birth defects and deformities among residents of the region.

Mitigation and Management

In an effort to manage the ecological disaster, five nations—Kazakhstan, the Kyrgyz Republic, Tajikistan, Turkmenistan, and Uzbekistan—agreed to work cooperatively in 1992 to restore the Aral Sea region. However, these same countries hold the agricultural lands that receive the water from the Syr Darya and Amu Darya rivers. If they stopped all water diversion, their agricultural sectors would collapse.

Before the five regional countries could begin their restoration work, a number of complex issues had to be negotiated. The Russian Academy of Sciences organized an international symposium on the Aral Sea, which was held in Nukus, Uzbekistan, in 1990. The Nukus Symposium featured over 200 scientists from twenty-seven countries. Up to forty separate reports were delivered over the four-day event.

One collaboration of scientists proposed creating an Aral Sea bank, which would require water users to pay for irrigation water taken from the Syr Darya and Amu Darya rivers. This system would use water prices to ensure the return of sufficient water to the Aral Sea. The concept, although environmentally feasible, was not considered politically acceptable. The symposium concluded with a broad agreement that the Aral Sea was in ecological crisis and that regional solutions needed to be developed.

By 1992, the same five nations in the region reached an agreement to create an Interstate Commission for Water Coordination (ICWC) to work toward common goals to restore the Aral Sea. The ICWC was charged with overseeing water allocation and fair irrigation practices for each country and with implementing projects to restore degraded portions of the Aral Sea. Although these regulatory measures were collectively drawn up, enforcement was delegated to each host country, which resulted in inadequate oversight.

From 1998 to 2003, The World Bank committed $21.5 million to address elements of the Aral Sea crisis. Through its Water and Environmental Management Project of the Aral Sea Basin Program, the Bank enlisted the leadership of the ICWC to set a number of goals, including reducing the salinity of the sea, improving agricultural water conservation practices to allow more water to run to the wetlands, and reducing the amount of irrigation upriver. This cooperative effort also was aimed at restoring wetlands in the lower Amu Darya River delta, particularly Lake Sudoche, which is a Ramsar Site of International Importance.

In 2001, Kazakhstan and Uzbekistan signed agreements with The World Bank for an $85.8 million project to build a dam and improve the water quality of the Aral Sea. The 8-mile-long (13-kilometer-long) Kok-Aral Dam, completed in 2005, sectioned off the Small Aral Sea to save a remaining portion of the Aral.

The dam's placement, in the middle of what was the Aral Sea before it began shrinking, meant abandonment of the goal of total restoration of the water resource and its associated wetland areas. By 2008, however, the Small Aral Sea to the north had grown by 30 percent. From 2005 to 2008, water depths increased from 98 feet (30 meters) to 137 feet (42 meters) and from 1,100 square miles (2,849 square kilometers) to 1,274 square miles (3,300 square kilometers). Salinity descended from 1.2 ounces (34 grams) per liter to less than 0.53 ounces (15.03 grams) with the influx of 350 million cubic feet (10 million cubic meters) of new water.

This project restored only an area less than a third of the size of the 1950s historical Aral Sea, which commonly featured salinity below 0.46 ounces (13 grams) and depths that exceeded 150 feet (46 meters). While the northern reaches of the basin filled with water, the southern and western areas continued to languish in a semi-arid and toxic condition.

For the first time in decades, however, signs of new wetlands were documented, as was the return of bird species to previously desolate areas. Due to better water conservation measures on farms, irrigation withdrawals upriver descended from a high of 28.1 trillion gallons (106.4 trillion liters) per year in

ARAL SEA PLANTS AND ANIMALS

Species Kind	Common Name	Scientific Name	Characteristics
Fish	Silver carp	*Hypophthalmichthys molitrix*	Known as "fat tongue" by Aral fisherman, this invasive species can leap from the water when scared and often weighs more than 42 pounds (19 kilograms).
Crustacean	Brine shrimp	*Artemia salina*	Able to withstand high salt conditions and lie dormant in dried seabeds, these crustaceans eat algae and provide essential food for many fish.
Plant	Saxaul	*Haloxylon ammodendron*	This shrub, indigenous to arid Central Asia, grows to 10 feet (3 meters) tall and helps stem erosion in dried lake beds.
Mammal	Corsac fox	*Vulpes corsac*	Relying on dens with multiple holes for safe shelter, this very social, medium-sized canine eats insects, reptiles, and small mammals.
Insect	Cladoceran	*Cladocera sp.*	Up to twelve varieties of this jumping water flea disappeared with vanishing waterways, but several have reappeared in newly flooded areas.
Bird	Dalmatian pelican	*Pelecanus crispus*	As wetland reed communities vanished due to receding waters, so did this large sea bird that relies on medium-sized fish for its daily sustenance.

1980 to 24.8 trillion gallons (93.9 trillion liters) per year in 2000. Two hatcheries, funded with grants from the United Nations and the government of Israel, released up to 30 million sturgeon, carp, and flounder by 2009. Despite this level of improvement, the port of Aral was still 7 miles (11 kilometers) from the water's edge in 2009.

The second component of The World Bank project, which was approved by Kazakhstan in 2009 but may not break ground until 2011, involves improving the irrigation inflow to the southern section of the Aral Sea. This $325.8 million project includes repairs to an existing dam and digging a new channel that eventually will connect the two divided bodies of water. While the goal of broader restoration of the Aral Sea may take two or more decades, the health of the delta region along the Syr Darya and Amu Darya rivers already has improved, with substantial regrowth of wetland species across the flooded areas.

Selected Web Sites

Aral Sea Loss and Cotton: http://www.american.edu/ted/aral.htm.
Food and Agriculture Organization of the United Nations: http://www.fao.org.
ICWC Aral Sea Information: http://www.icwc-aral.uz.
LakeNet, World Lakes Network: htpp://www.worldlakes.org.
Overview on Aral Sea: http://www.cawater-info.net/aral/index_e.htm.

Further Reading

Dukhovny, V.A. *The Aral Sea: Past, Present, and Future.* Tashkent, Uzbekistan: Interstate Commission for Water Coordination, 2008.

Ferguson, Rob. *The Devil and the Disappearing Sea.* Vancouver, Canada: Raincoast, 2003.

Michlin, Philip. "Water in the Aral Sea Basin of Central Asia: Cause of Conflict or Cooperation?" *Eurasian Geography and Economics* 43:7 (2002): 505–528.

Morimoto, Yukihiro. "The Pelican Scenario for Nature Restoration of the Aral Sea Wetland Ecosystems." *Landscape and Ecological Engineering,* Tokyo, Japan, 2005.

Roll, Gulnara. *Aral Sea: Experience and Lessons Learned.* Washington, DC: World Bank, 2006.

United Nations Educational, Scientific, and Cultural Organization. *Water Related Vision for the Aral Sea Basin.* Paris, France: UNESCO, 2000.

9 Izembek National Wildlife Refuge Alaska

The Izembek wetlands are a remote subarctic coastal ecosystem located on the Alaskan Peninsula. The area designated in 1960 as the Izembek National Wildlife Refuge consists of 650 square miles (1,684 square kilometers), or 416,000 acres (168,349 hectares), of nearly treeless habitat, including mountains, active volcanoes, glaciers, foothills, upland meadows, freshwater lakes and rivers, thermal springs, and expansive wetlands. It is bordered by water on two sides, with the Bering Sea on the north and the Pacific Ocean on the south. Izembek is roughly 634 miles (1,020 kilometers) southwest of the City of Anchorage.

The refuge contains 279 square miles (723 square kilometers), or 178,560 acres (72,261 hectares), of wetlands. Protected by a series of barrier islands, these wetlands are characterized by rich plant systems and prolific bird breeding grounds. The most common wetland type is the coastal lagoon that spans 150 square miles (389 square kilometers), or 93,371 acres (37,786 hectares), of saltwater habitat. Vegetation within the lagoon is dominated by a dense forest of marine eelgrass (*Zostera marina*), the largest bed of its kind in North America.

The Izembek Lagoon features shallow brackish waters and a barrier beach. The beach provides physical protection from the ocean, reduces storm impacts, and allows the protected waters, warmed by sunlight, to support a diversity of species. The central eelgrass beds form a unique ecosystem: long, fragile grass blades create a dense, floating mass that filters water, serves as protective habitat for young fish and clams, and provides large amounts of food for waterfowl. Surrounding the lagoon are marshes and wet meadows composed of lyme grass

(*Elymus arenaria*) and several species of sedges (*Carex sp.*). The area supports a bird population that can exceed 500,000 birds in a given year.

The weather in the Alaskan Peninsula is typically cold, wet, and windy. With steady winds around 20 miles per hour (32 kilometers per hour) and gusts above 50 miles per hour (80 kilometers per hour), the subarctic temperature rarely climbs above 70 degrees Fahrenheit (21 degrees Celsius) with winter temperatures often below 0 degrees Fahrenheit (-18 degrees Celsius).

There are thirty-nine species of fish that inhabit the Izembek waters, including walleye (*Theragra chalcogramma*), herring (*Clupea harengus*), and cod (*Gadus macrocephalus*). A common fish is the Chinook salmon (*Oncorhynchus tshawytscha*). These salmon number in the millions and return to their birthplace upriver to spawn before they die.

The Chinook, coho (*Oncorhynchus kisutch*), and pink salmon (*Oncorhynchus gorbuscha*) are staple foods of the brown bear (*Ursus arctos horribilis*), a resident that primarily feeds on fish and berries in the summer months in preparation for hibernation during the winter. Weighing up to 1,600 pounds (726 kilograms) these bears are apex predators, residing at the top of their food chain and hunted only by humans. Mature brown bears stand over 6 feet (1.8 meters) tall on their

During the mating season, Steller sea lions (*Eumetopias jubatus*) gather in rookeries like this one. The number of these sea lions is dwindling due to commercial overfishing of their primary food source—fish species such as herring, pollock, and salmon. (© Alexander/Fotolia)

rear legs and can be very aggressive, especially when a mother's young cubs are threatened.

The gray wolf (*Canus lupus*) stalks the open grasses and meadows in search of small prey in summer. Each autumn, packs of up to a dozen wolves hunt for larger game such as the caribou (*Rangifer tarandus*). More than 54,000 caribou migrate into the refuge from their northern calving grounds when the weather cools.

Steller sea lions (*Eumetopias jubatus*), the largest of the species, occupy the cold waters. Weighing 50 pounds (23 kilograms) at birth, these sea lions feed on their mother's rich milk and then thrive on an ample supply of fish. Adult males grow up to a massive 2,400 pounds (1,089 kilograms).

The local winter population of birds exceeds 23,000, and nearly half a million birds, more than eighty-two species, live in the wetlands during the summer months. The threatened Steller's eider (*Polysticta stelleri*), a small marine duck, spends its days in the lagoons, diving underwater for short periods in search of small clams. The estimated 130,000 brant (*Branta bernicla*) and 62,000 emperor geese (*Philacte canagica*) that visit the area during their spring and fall migrations also feed on submerged vegetation in the lagoons.

The Izembek Refuge is situated near prominent volcanoes, including the 9,373-foot (2.857-meter) Shishaldin Volcano, one of the most active in the Aleutian mountain range. Located about 680 miles (1,094 kilometers) southwest of Anchorage, near the center of Unimak Island, Shishaldin is a symmetric stratovolcano that forms the highest peak in the Aleutian Islands.

Shishaldin erupted twenty-eight times during the nineteenth and twentieth centuries, including eruptions in 1995, 1999, and 2004. The largest of its eruptions in the past 175 years occurred on April 19, 1999, when the volcano spewed a 45,000-foot (13,716-meter) column of steam and debris that could be seen from 100 miles (160 kilometers) away; basaltic lava flowed down the northern flank of the mountain, covering everything in its path with several feet of new rock.

In 2009, the volcano released a visible plume of steam from its conical peak every few months. Adjacent tectonic pressure also continues to trigger earthquakes; most are below the magnitude of 1 (on a scale of 1 to 10) and last up to 2 minutes.

Human Uses

Small groups of Alaskan natives, called Aleutians, have occupied the Izembek area since 3000 B.C.E. Historians theorize that these people descend from Asiatic groups that crossed the Bering Straight land bridge around 5,000 to 15,000 years ago. Archaeological sites in the Izembek region have provided evidence of 9,000-year-old shelters that were set up during summer months for toolmaking and for the processing of game and seafood.

Most of these early explorers continued on toward the heart of North America, but some settled in Alaska. The peoples who stayed in the region were dependent on the coastal ecosystem and relied on the rich marine wildlife for almost all of their needs, including food, clothing, and fuel.

Spanish explorers arrived in 1741 and found a land of both intense harshness—with cold months dominating more than three-quarters of the year—and spectacular beauty. When Russian explorers wintered in a nearby bay in 1761, they named the coastal area Izembek after the ship's doctor, Karl Izembek. Under Russian occupation between 1780 and 1820, thousands of the native Aleuts perished from disease and conflict, and they were forced to consolidate their settlements from 169 to thirty-nine. By the 1830s, their population had been decimated from 25,000 to 2,000. Finding the land too difficult to settle, Russia sold the Aleutian Islands to the United States in 1867. The following century saw the Aleut people recover; by 2001, their population was 11,941.

As of 2004, Izembek's regional population was about 2,629 (37 percent were Aleuts), spread across an area called the Aleutians East Borough—a 15,012-square-mile (38,881-square-kilometer) expanse that includes 8,020 miles (12,904 kilometers) of saltwater habitats. The village of Cold Bay sits next to the Izembek National Wildlife Refuge. During World War II, it hosted Fort Randall, a U.S. military base; up to 20,000 soldiers were stationed here in 1945. With just ninety-four residents in 2009, it now features an airport, a community center, a weather station, a few businesses, and a visitor center for the refuge.

Long-distance plane traffic used to stop in Cold Bay for refueling until the 1970s when jets with greater distance capacity replaced propeller planes. Today, the main use of the remaining 10,420-foot-long (3,176-meters-long) airfield is for regional traffic and emergency landings for planes crossing the Pacific Ocean.

Pollution and Damage

Approximately 47 percent of western Alaska's 355 million acres (144 million hectares) has been classified as wetlands. The Izembek wetlands underwent considerable stress in the twentieth century from a range of natural and human factors.

Scientists estimate that Alaska has lost 1 percent (1,668,500 acres, or 675,218 hectares) of its wetlands over the last 100 years. About 30,000 acres (12,141 hectares) of wetlands in western Alaska have been lost to oil and gas mining since the 1990s. Other wetlands have been damaged by various forestry practices, human settlement, and the development of transportation systems.

Volcanic eruption and earthquake activity are ongoing threats to the Izembek wetlands. During the twentieth century, in addition to Shishaldin, the nearby volcanoes Amak (1,683 feet, or 513 meters), Pavlof (8,261 feet, or 2,518 meters), and Frosty (6,299 feet, or 1,920 meters) were all active. Frosty had the biggest volcanic eruption in the region a few thousand years ago, sending lava, rock fragments, and gas across hundreds of miles.

The most recent eruption was from Shishaldin in 2004, when it emitted lava and plumes of steam and ash thousands of feet into the air, as well as powerful odors of sulfur. Over a period of two months, the volcano also triggered earthquakes lasting up to six minutes in length. The volcanic activity upset the delicate wetland ecosystem, especially through the deposition of several inches of fine volcanic ash debris on top of vegetation.

Although commercial oil drilling has been performed in the Bering Sea since 1902, new onshore oil/gas extraction leases for areas north and east of the refuge were signed in 2005. Onshore oil drilling operations require extraction equipment, heavy machinery, pipelines, roads, and storage facilities that potentially threaten wetlands.

Another danger is the passage of supertanker boats that carry oil from northern Alaska through the Bering Strait to other countries. If a ship were to spill oil, such as the 987-foot (301-meter) *Exxon Valdez* did in 1989 in Prince William Sound in the Gulf of Alaska, spilling 11 million gallons (42 million liters) of crude oil, the results would be devastating to the wetlands and wildlife. The *Exxon Valdez* accident was estimated to have resulted in the deaths of 250,000 seabirds, 3,000 sea otters, 300 harbor seals, 250 bald eagles, twenty-two killer whales, and several billion fish.

MILITARY CONTAMINATION ESTIMATES AT IZEMBEK NATIONAL WILDLIFE REFUGE

Chemical	Amount Used per Year in Gallons	Estimated Spillage Amount, as a Percent	Total Estimated Spillage Amounts, in Gallons
Diesel	280,000	0.1	5,320
Oils	2,000	10	3,800
Antifreeze	100	10	190
Pesticides	50	10	95
Paint thinner	50	10	95
Battery acid	20	50	180
PCB liquids	unknown	50	200

Source: U.S. Fish and Wildlife Service, 2004.

In 2004, the U.S. Fish and Wildlife Service (FWS) prepared a report documenting the contamination of portions of the Izembek Refuge by Fort Randall, run by the U.S. Army and the U.S. Air Force between 1942 and 1950, and chronicled the collective cleanup efforts by the federal government and local communities. When the base closed, the entire campus and its contents were left to decay, including an incinerator and up to 3,000 55-gallon (208-liter) drums holding fuel, pesticides, deicing agents, and other toxic chemicals.

Other unused or waste materials were buried in several locations. The report estimates that 300 acres (121 hectares) of trash were not properly disposed of and were leaching pollutants into groundwater aquifers. By 1994, large fuel tanks were removed from the waterfront area and runway, and venting systems were installed to clean the nearby soils in 1997. In 1998, the incinerator was demolished and buried on-site.

By 2000, up to 2,250 55-gallon (208-liter) drums had been removed with tons of the surrounding soil. Researchers have identified petroleum compounds and pesticides in the soil, and additional soil remediation projects were under way as of 2010.

Evidence of ocean pollution has become more apparent in Alaska since the 1980s. Large amounts of trash, especially floating plastic, kill hundreds of coastal birds a year, as the birds mistake the brightly colored material for food and ingest it or get tangled in it and drown.

Scientists also are documenting evidence of climate change in Alaska, as polar regions warm at unprecedented rates. Between 1949 and 2006, the Alaska Climate Research Center reported that the average air temperature increased by 3.4 degrees Fahrenheit (15.9 degrees Celsius). Regional warming has resulted in water level increases up to 3 inches (7.6 centimeters), submerging land and changing wetland footprints.

Mitigation and Management

The Izembek National Wildlife Refuge has been well protected through a number of conservation actions. In 1972, the state of Alaska recognized a portion of the wetlands lagoon as a game refuge. In 1980, in an effort to further protect the wetlands, the U.S. Congress designated 300,000 acres (121,406 hectares) as a federal wilderness under the Alaska National Interest Lands Conservation Act. In 1986, the Izembek National Wildlife Refuge became the first site in the United States to be designated a Ramsar Site of International Importance.

Although a conservationist approach exists among some sectors of the local community, others, including native and community leaders, have lobbied for the development of the region. Paving a road through the Izembek Refuge, from Cold Bay (population 81) to King Cove (population 807), became a national issue in 1998, as the U.S. Congress supported the project with $40 million in funding. Supporters included Alaska Senator Ted Stevens and the King Cove Corporation, an Aleutian company that proposed a land exchange of 96 square miles (249 square kilometers) of a combination of private King Cove Corporation and Alaskan state lands for the 27-mile-long (43-kilometer-long), one-third-mile-wide (.53-kilometer-wide) roadway between the two towns. The precedent of constructing such a road through a federal wilderness area drew protest from environmentalists and many Aleuts.

As a compromise, Congress appropriated $37.5 million in 2007 under the King Cove Health and Safety Act for improvements to the King Cove medical clinic and airport and to fund a marine transportation system link, a hovercraft, between the two cities. The 98-foot (30-meter) hovercraft, unfortunately, often was unable to transport emergency medical passengers due to rough water; in addition, it was too expensive for the local government to cover its operating costs. After continued debate, in March 2009, Congress passed the Izembek and Alaska Peninsula Refuge Enhancement Act, which established a process to increase the size of the federal wilderness areas by more than 61,000 acres (24,686 hectares) in exchange for a small, gravel single-lane road leading from King Cove to the Cold Bay airport. Conservation groups, such as the Friends of Alaska National Wildlife Refuges and the Wilderness Society, strongly oppose

IZEMBEK NATIONAL WILDLIFE REFUGE COMPLEX LAND PROTECTION PLAN

The objective of the plan was to answer the following questions:

1. What are the private lands within the Izembek complex
2. What resources are we trying to protect
3. What methods do we have for resource protection
4. How does the FWS set priorities for resource protection, and what are these priorities
5. What land protection measures do we recommend
6. How might the FWS protection priorities affect private landowners and others

the road project and have asked the U.S. Interior Department to halt the project—a requirement to obtain an environmental impact statement—as they feel that it goes against the public interest of the refuge.

In 1998, the FWS developed the Izembek National Wildlife Refuge Complex Land Protection Plan. The plan included the Izembek National Wildlife Refuge and additional surrounding national wildlife refuges, including the Alaska Peninsula National Wildlife Refuge and Unimak Island of the Alaska Maritime Refuge, totaling 2.9 million acres (1.2 million hectares). Of the 2.5 million acres (1.1 million hectares) of surface lands protected, private landowners held titles or claims to approximately 989,267 acres (400,342 hectares), or about 39 percent.

The plan emphasized the fact that wildlife does not follow borders, and in order to better manage the region, all landowners—federal, state, and private—must cooperate to protect the area. The plan also stated that cooperation should be voluntary and based on mutual consent. This type of a document typically is revised every ten to fifteen years.

Selected Web Sites

Alaska Department of Fish and Game Wildlife Conservation: http://www.wildlife.alaska.gov.

Alaska Volcano Observatory: http://www.avo.alaska.edu.

Aleutians Regional Site: http://www.aleutianseast.org.

Izembek National Wildlife Refuge: http://izembek.fws.gov.

The Wilderness Society "Map of Izembek": http://wilderness.org/content/izembek-national-wildlife-refuge-map.

Further Reading

Murphy, Michael. "A Comparison of Fish Assemblages in Eelgrass and Adjacent Sub-Tidal Habitats Near Craig, Alaska." *Alaska Fishery Research Bulletin*, Volume 7, 2000.

Ramsar Convention on Wetlands. *Site Summary: Izembek Lagoon National Wildlife Refuge*. Gland, Switzerland: Ramsar Convention, 2003.

———. *Wetlands and the Izembek FishMap Program*. Gland, Switzerland: Ramsar Convention, 2006.

U.S. Fish and Wildlife Service. *Izembek National Wildlife Refuge Complex*. Washington, DC: U.S. Department of the Interior, 2004.

10 | Kopuatai Peat Dome
New Zealand

The Kopuatai Peat Dome is the largest inland freshwater wetland in New Zealand, an independent country consisting of two main landmasses (the North Island and the South Island) and several smaller islands, in the southwest Pacific Ocean. Measuring 40 square miles (104 square kilometers) in size, the dome is bounded by the main channels of the Piako and Waihou rivers in the low-lying Hauraki Plains of the central North Island.

The peat dome is made up of a several-thousand-year-old thick web of vegetation that floats on a shallow pond. The cool temperate zone of northern New Zealand receives approximately 44 inches (112 centimeters) of rain per year, and the shallow wetland waters range from 3 to 6 feet (0.9 to 1.8 meters) in depth.

The Kopuatai Peat Dome began to form about 14,000 years ago. It was part of a larger freshwater wetland that once stretched to nearly 100 square miles (259 square kilometers), two and a half times Kopuatai's present size. In addition, this wetland was connected to another wetland to the north, the Firth of Thames.

Although total wetlands across New Zealand are estimated at 176 square miles (456 square kilometers), Kopuatai is the only peat dome remaining in the country. The land around the wetland is flat, and there are few higher vantage points. Travel into the area is difficult, as there are no roads, though several man-made water channels exist. These factors have helped protect the Kopuatai Peat Dome as an isolated wetland. While its borders have been degraded by human development, the center of the area has been mostly untouched.

Rivers, ponds, marshes, swampland, and lagoons surround the Kopuatai Peat Dome. The wetland's hydrology and ecology play a key role in flood protection of the surrounding uplands.

The wetland's water is oligotrophic, having a deficiency of plant nutrients and an abundance of dissolved oxygen. With its very slow breakdown of plant and animal material, the detritus (loose material that results directly from disintegration) forms into ever-increasing layers that are preserved for thousands of years. At the heart of the Kopuatai wetland, the peat is 40 feet (12.2 meters) deep and 7 feet (2.1 meters) thick around the edges.

New Zealand's native vegetation is 80 percent endemic (unique to the country), due to the country's geographical isolation, and the Kopuatai Peat Dome hosts more than 100 species of plants, nine of which are threatened. For instance, on the southern edge of the wetland is a 44-acre (18-hectare) stand of kahikatea trees (*Dacrycarpus dacrydioides*). These conifers are the tallest native trees on the island, growing to a height of 180 feet (55 meters), and they thrive in moist soils. Kopuatai also is only one of three locations in New Zealand that contains a family of rush-like flowering plants called restiads. These herbaceous plants are known for their fast-growing stems and tufted, stacked flowers.

The heart of the peat dome features standing water and more than 5,430 acres (2,197 hectares) of grasses, sedges, and rushes. The greater jointed rush (*Sporadanthus traversiis*) is common. The low-growing club moss (*Lycopodium serpentinum*) forms the basis of the peat structure.

BIRDS OF THE KOPUATAI PEAT DOME

Common Name	Scientific Name	Characteristics
Australasian bittern	*Botaurus poiciloptilus*	Heard more often than seen due to its distinctively loud call, this medium-sized, mostly nocturnal wetland bird feeds on frogs and fish.
Fernbird	*Bowdleria punctata*	This threatened, tiny, secretive bird has small wings and lives in grassy wet meadows.
Baillon's crake	*Porzana pusilla*	An elusive wetland species, this marsh bird lives deep in inaccessible swampland, nesting just inches above water levels on a thin bed of dried grass.
White heron	*Egretta alba modesta*	Often roosting in trees with other family members, this rare marsh bird stalks the edges of wetlands for small fish and other vertebrates, such as frogs or small snakes.

Source: New Zealand Ministry for the Environment, 2008.

Up to fifty-four species of birds live in Kopuatai. Due to their shrinking habitat, the federal government has protected twenty-seven of them.

The wetland's lack of dry ground makes it a challenge for most mammals to survive. In fact, New Zealand has no native mammals, other than bat, seal, and dolphin species. As the nonnative mammal numbers have increased over the twentieth century, invasive species, such as possums, feral cats, rodents, and wild pigs, have roamed the Kopuatai Peat Dome and have threatened native bird populations.

Inside the heart of the wetland are pockets of open water, which is prime habitat for several fish species, including the black mudfish (*Neochanna diversus*) and the long-finned eel (*Anguilla dieffenbachia*). Introduced species, such as the goldfish, brown bullhead, and mosquito fish, have taken over much of the freshwater habitat.

A resident invertebrate, the orb-weaver spider (*Eriophora heroine*), is well known for its large, spiral, wheel-shaped webs. The wetland also contains several amphibians, such as two endemic species of frogs: Hochstetter's frog (*Leiopelma hochstetteri*) and Archey's frog (*Leiopelma archeyi*).

Human Uses

The Maori people, whose name translates into the word "natural," are the natives of New Zealand. They arrived on the island around 800 C.E. Migrating from eastern Polynesia in small groups of dugout canoes, the Maori numbered around 100,000 in 1769.

Small tribes lived in relative harmony with the wetlands, and both inland freshwater and coastal habitats were used for growing vegetables and fruits, fishing, hunting, and food gathering. At Kopuatai, the Maori fished in the open waters, grew crops adjacent to the wetlands in its rich soils, harvested peat for bedding and fuel, used kahikatea trees to build structures, wove flax grasses into clothing, mats, and ropes, and hunted for birds—many types of feathers were used as sacred ornamental headwear.

In 1840, Great Britain took control of the islands, and the subsequent loss of the Maori lands reduced their population to 42,113 by 1896. Since the 1960s, however, the Maori tribes have undergone a revival and regrowth. Today, the Maori account for 14 percent of New Zealand's 4.1 million citizens (roughly 565,000) and are integrated into the larger culture. Approximately 96 percent of the Maori live on the country's North Island.

New Zealand's population grew from 1.4 million in 1926 to 4 million in 2000, and this growth resulted in record development across both of the main islands. The area near the peat dome is primarily rural, with around 5,000 residents. What regional growth there has been has translated into more land

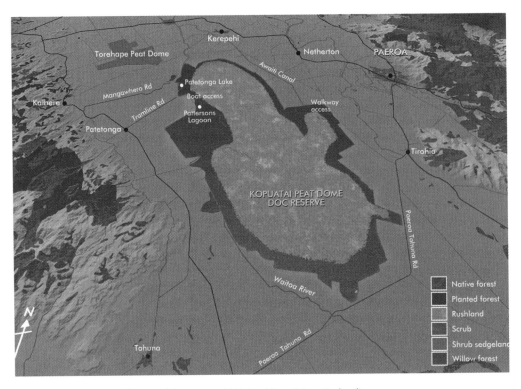

Legend:
- Native forest
- Planted forest
- Rushland
- Scrub
- Shrub sedgeland
- Willow forest

Source: Environment Waikato and the National Wetland Trust (New Zealand).

being used for building and farming and more water being diverted for drinking and irrigation. Population growth also has led to increased waste from septic systems, farming operations, roads, and residential and commercial buildings. Additional pavement has meant more impervious surfaces, and this has resulted in an increase in storm water runoff from adjacent streets, with oil, salts, nutrients, and trash polluting waterways and, eventually, wetlands.

At the time of European settlement, forests rich in kahikatea trees were one of New Zealand's most distinctive natural features. In the southern portion of the peat dome, tens of thousands of acres of old-growth stands were logged between 1885 and 1940 for a number of construction and manufacturing uses. For example, lightweight boxes used to store butter were a common product, with 56-pound (25-kilogram) slabs packaged in the strong, odorless wood. Less than 2 percent of the original stands of kahikatea trees remains on the North Island.

Pollution and Damage

Like many other countries, New Zealand viewed its wetland environment as a resource to be used for economic gain. At the turn of the twentieth century,

Kopuatai Peat Dome was viewed as a wasteland due to its peculiar hydrology, dense vegetation, and inaccessibility. By 1908, the government had implemented plans to drain 98,000 acres (39,659 hectares) of the peat dome using a series of man-made channels and floodgates. By 1930, more than 621 miles (999 kilometers) of canals had been dug and 93 miles (150 kilometers) of pathways constructed to access the canals.

Much of the drained or filled lands was cultivated as farms. The remaining peat bogs began to die, and up to half of the original wetlands were lost. Simultaneously, the populations of invasive wildlife, such as the nonnative brushtail possum (*Trichosurus arnhemensis*), originally introduced into the country for its fur, expanded and put pressure on fragile vegetation and bird nests that sit directly on wetland grasses. Species such as the Australasian bittern (*Botaurus poiciloptilus*), the buff-banded rail (*Gallirallus philippensis*), and the Baillon's crake (*Porzana pusilla*) declined sharply in population without the added protective space.

The Kopuatai Peat Dome wetlands rely on a steady supply of groundwater. Growth in farming in the region has resulted in increasing water removals from the nearby Piako River. The river's summer flow is especially low because manmade canals are opened to irrigate fields, leaving only a trickle to run into the wetlands. Kopuatai's reduced size since the 1980s is a result of this irregular

NEW ZEALAND WETLAND LOSSES

- Between 1954 and 1976, due to aggressive farm subsidies, approximately 29,650 acres (11,999 hectares) of wetlands were lost annually, amounting to a total of 652,355 acres (263,999 hectares) lost in a twenty-two-year period.

- Approximately 75 percent of New Zealand's wetlands are smaller than 2.5 acres (1 hectare) in size.

- Flood control structures, water removals, farm expansion, and pollution have eliminated 91 percent of the original wetlands, or more than 1,562 square miles (4,046 square kilometers).

- The remaining 9 percent of the original wetlands is in a degraded state, suffering from land development, water removal, and heavy pollution.

inflow of water. When less freshwater flows into the wetlands, vegetation dies off, starting at the edges; one obvious sign is patches of browned grasses and sedges appearing early in the summer.

Up to 95 percent of the Kopuatai Peat Dome was covered by native vegetation in 1840. As of the early twenty-first century, this figure had decreased by 15 percent as a result of development, reduced water flow, and other factors. Aggressive nonnative vegetation, such as common cord grass (*Spartina anglica*), with its dense roots and wide grass blades, choke out other plants from the wetland.

Mitigation and Management

In 1976, New Zealand joined the Ramsar Convention and made a commitment to protect its national wetlands. In 1979, a public and private working group assembled to discuss the health and status of the Kopuatai Peat Dome. The group of New Zealanders agreed to place a twenty-year moratorium on all human development at the site to better assess its health and to allow for restoration efforts. No regulations were applied to the adjacent lands or waterways

In 1987, the New Zealand Parliament passed the Conservation Act, which preserves the country's natural and historic resources. The act established the

HAURAKI DISTRICT COUNCIL'S GOALS FOR THE KOPUATAI PEAT DOME

- To preserve and protect the botanical and wildlife values and the natural character of the Wetland Conservation Zone.
- To maintain the flood control functions of the wetlands.
- To recognize the education, economic, and scientific roles of the wetlands.
- To promote the efficient conservation management of the wetlands.
- To promote a cooperative approach with the Department of Conservation concerning resource management issues within or affecting the zone.

Department of Conservation, unifying within one department the conservation functions formerly managed by five different government agencies.

For the first time in the country's history, newly established Wetland Management Reserves protected the wetlands. The department banned entry to the Kopuatai Peat Dome without a permit, as walking across the fragile floating vegetation causes immediate damage to the plants below. A series of historic waterfowl hunting huts were brought under the purview of the department, with strict management requirements, as were a number of artificial ponds that were built in the 1950s to draw waterfowl for hunting.

In 1989, the Kopuatai Peat Dome was designated a Ramsar Site of International Importance. In the report completed that same year, a note under the category of "adverse threats" was added: "The most serious threat to the wetland, particularly the mineralized wetland areas, is continuing drainage of the surrounding area."

The Kopuatai Peat Dome is under the local jurisdiction of the Hauraki District Council, a government body, which includes the towns of Paeroa on the eastern border and Patetonga on the western border. Although the national government owns the entire site, the surrounding upland and wetland areas are privately held, making management and watershed protection complicated.

In 1997, the Hauraki District Council declared the Kopuatai Peat Dome a Wetland Conservation Zone, which offers a level of regional resource protection. A number of goals were set with this designation.

Since the 1980s, New Zealand's national government has strengthened its stance on wetlands protection and recognized the importance of these areas as part of its national cultural heritage and identity. In 2007, the national budget for ecological wetland restorations increased tenfold, to $2 million per year. This funding has been used to develop collaborative partnerships between regional councils, landowners, farmers, and conservation groups.

Although the international norm has been for governments to purchase and set aside large amounts of land for conservation, New Zealand has a higher percentage of wetlands under private ownership than many other countries. Private and public funding in 2005 allocated $2.3 million to thirty-eight wetland restoration projects and, in 2006, $1.7 million was dedicated to fifty-three sites.

The Kopuatai Peat Dome underwent considerable habitat loss in the twentieth century from human dredging and drainage projects, farming, and development. Restoring diverted waters and rebuilding lost habitat is projected to take years of commitment and oversight. In addition, government officials and wetland managers have the dual challenge of protecting the wetlands and convincing the public of the value of preserving these natural resources.

At the World Wetlands Day Conservation Awards in 2001, Marion Hobbs of the New Zealand Department of Fish and Game, summed up the primary challenge of managing the nation's wetlands:

> Unlike forests you cannot just put a fence around them and leave them to look after themselves. From the day they are created they [wetlands] start to die. They are always in the process of evolving towards dry land.

Selected Web Sites

Maori Culture: http://www.maori.info.
National Wetland Trust of New Zealand: http://www.wetlandtrust.org.nz.
New Zealand Department of Conservation: http://www.doc.govt.nz.

Further Reading

Environment Waikato Association. *Restoring Waikato's Indigenous Biodiversity.* Waikato, New Zealand: Waikato Biodiversity Forum, 2006.

Hunt, Janet. *Wetlands of New Zealand.* New York: Random House, 2007.

Moon, Geoff. *New Zealand Wetland Birds and Their World.* French's Forest, Australia: New Holland Books, 2009.

New Zealand Ministry for the Environment. *Getting in on the Act: An Everyday Guide to the Resource Management Act of 1991.* Wellington, New Zealand, 2006.

———. *The State of New Zealand's Environment: The State of Our Waters.* Wellington, New Zealand, 2006.

WETLANDS
CONCLUSION

11 Wetland Challenges and Solutions

Although the late twentieth and early twenty-first centuries witnessed a global recognition of the environmental benefits that wetland ecosystems offer, difficult hurdles remain to manage and protect these sensitive and critical resource areas. The worldwide human population growth of 82.8 million people per year is paramount among the many challenges of wetland preservation. Fragmented approaches to water resources management and wetland protection exist both within and among most nations.

The preservation of wetlands therefore requires a multidisciplinary approach that reaches across borders and integrates the technical, economic, environmental, social, and legal aspects of wildlife and water management philosophies. Cooperation between policymakers, government agencies, researchers, and communities is vital for the health and long-term survival of wetlands.

Population Pressures

Demographers and mathematicians question what the future holds for a global population that reached 6.7 billion in 2009. The United Nations stated that growth on a global scale decreased slightly from a high of 2.19 percent annually in 1963 to 1.16 percent in 2008. Countries such as Japan and Russia, and areas such as Western Europe, are projected to shrink in population (up to 14 percent by 2050) due to low birthrates.

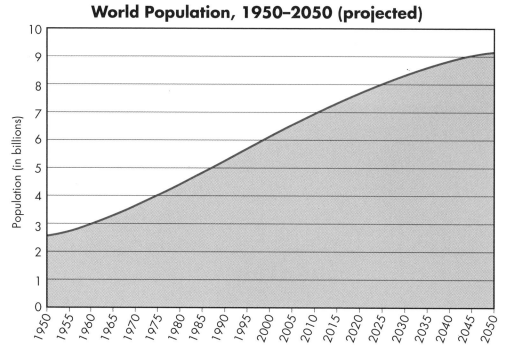

World Population, 1950–2050 (projected)

Source: United Nations Environment Program.

Despite a slowing of the growth rate in certain regions, however, the total world population is predicted to increase considerably in the twenty-first century. The United Nations estimates that the world will reach a population of 8 billion by 2028. In 2009, China, India, and Malaysia accounted for 60 percent of the total planetary population and were projected to be the areas of fastest growth.

Conservationists and government agencies alike debate whether or not a growing population and wetland protection goals can coexist. The evidence of the effectiveness of wetland conservation programs that began in the mid-twentieth century is mixed.

In the United States, a no net loss policy for wetlands was set by Congress in 1989 with the target of creating 100,000 new acres (40,469 hectares) per year by 2005. Despite reaching this goal, a 1998 federal government survey found a simultaneous problem: up to 130,480 acres (52,803 hectares) of wetlands were lost per year from 1986 to 1997. By 2005, the U.S. Environmental Protection Agency estimated that a plan to restore up to 200,000 acres (80,937 hectares) per year could be implemented, but there would still be 100,000 acres (40,469 hectares) lost per year. Thus a net gain of only 100,000 acres (40,469 hectares) of wetlands per year would result.

The Society of Wetland Scientists, a Virginia-based international organization that works toward fostering sound wetland science, management, and education, questioned the accuracy of these surveys, pointing to a lack of government oversight, as well as the regulatory hypocrisy of continuing to permit losses.

A 2008 report by the U.S. Fish and Wildlife Service (FWS) calculated that 1.1 million acres (450,000 hectares) of wetlands had been restored since 2004, and an additional 1 million acres (400,000 hectares) were protected. However, the FWS report did not mention how many acres still were being lost each year.

Although strides in better wetland management and protection have been recorded in both the United States and other countries, continuing development pressures have made the policy of no net losses difficult to implement and enforce.

Wetland Treaties and Agreements

Since the late twentieth century, a number of international accords have been implemented to protect wetlands. By working across borders and recognizing the value of collective efforts, international agreements have brought thousands of ecological regions to the attention of the public as valuable natural resource areas.

Such agreements not only elevate the status of wetlands as an environmental asset but also install a global system of checks and balances. By using unified standards established under treaties and agreements, the countries involved are better able to work together to protect and preserve wetland habitats.

Ramsar Convention Challenges

The 1971 Ramsar Convention, the preeminent global treaty for the conservation and sustainable use of wetland areas, has a staff of fourteen and an annual budget of approximately $3.4 million (as of 2009), based on funds contributed by member nations. The success of the convention relies on voluntary membership and the willingness of each member country to commit resources to manage specific areas.

In some countries, a range of persistent problems occurs, including illegal fishing and hunting, damage to wetland vegetation through alteration and filling, pollution runoff, water removals, and occupation by humans within the identified sites. To date, Ramsar members have not developed a regulatory enforcement mechanism. Each country is currently responsible for adhering to its original commitments—made in writing upon joining the convention—to enforce wetland protection within its boundaries. Local citizens and environmental organizations sometimes reveal and report noncompliance.

Under this voluntary structure, no protected wetlands have been severely damaged. Despite there being 583,680 square miles (over 1.5 million square kilometers) of such "protected" wetlands, this number is only about 10 percent of the world's total, which was estimated at 4.9 million square miles (12.7 million square kilometers) in 2005.

One example of a threatened Ramsar site is the Gwydir River Wetland in northern Australia. Despite being designated as a protected wetland since 1999 and subsequently subject to strict federal government oversight, in 2007, a local farmer bulldozed 1,853 acres (750 hectares) of the wetland before someone reported the damage. Under a 2003 Australian law, which was modeled after Ramsar guidelines, the farmer faced steep fines of up to $810,000 (in U.S. dollars), but no jail time.

North American Waterfowl Management Plan

Like the Ramsar Convention, the 1986 North American Waterfowl Management Plan aims to protect wetlands, although the scope of the plan is only between three countries—Canada, Mexico, and the United States.

Recognizing the importance of waterfowl and wetlands to North America and the need for international cooperation to assist in the recovery of wildlife populations, the U.S. and Canadian governments developed a strategy to restore waterfowl populations through habitat protection. The strategy was outlined in the North American Waterfowl Management Plan, which was signed in 1986 by Canada and the United States. Mexico became a signatory when the plan was updated in 1994.

The plan relies upon implementation at the federal, state, provincial, tribal, and local levels. Its success is dependent upon the strength of partnerships, considered joint ventures, in which various government sectors, businesses, conservation organizations, and individual citizens work together. Such joint ventures develop implementation plans for protecting waterfowl and conserving specific wetland habitats.

By 2006, at least sixteen joint ventures had invested $4.5 billion to protect or restore 15.7 million acres (6.4 million hectares) of waterfowl habitat. Similar to Ramsar members, North American Waterfowl Management Plan leaders rely on volunteer commitments from each country involved. Cultural differences, funding variances, language differences, large geographical divides, and varying goals among the three countries have posed challenges to implementing the conservation plan. Each government faces its own particular challenges in protecting and preserving its wetlands—such as economic growth, expansion of agriculture, pollution, and invasive species—making its goal implementation unique.

Status reports prepared by plan members in the mid-2000s revealed ongoing challenges. For example, while the populations of northern shoveler (*Anas*

The name of the northern pintail duck (*Anas acuta*) is derived from its long, narrow, pointed tail. This species lives in the wetlands of Asia, northern Europe, and North America. During colder months, these ducks migrate south as far as the equator. *(David Tipling/The Image Bank/Getty Images)*

clypeata), gadwall (*Anas strepera*), and green-winged teal (*Anas carolinensis*) ducks have shown impressive regrowth, the numbers for species such as the greater scaup (*Aythya marila*) and northern pintail (*Anas acuta*) have fallen below recovery expectations. The latter two species are considered critical indicators to the health of wetlands because they only live where water quality is good and ample vegetation is present. The pintail, in particular, is in decline, with populations estimated at 54 percent under plan goals.

Surveys also found an 11 percent reduction in the total number of ducks from 2003 to 2004, and another drop of 9 percent in the mallard (*Anas platyhynchos*) breeding population in 2005. In order to protect these and other waterfowl species, the three nations must continue to assert proactive strategies to improve their wetland habitats.

Wetland Publications

Thanks to international efforts throughout the past century, an impressive body of knowledge about wetlands has been accumulated. The scientific community has proven with hard evidence that a wetland is a reservoir of bountiful life.

Water held by the land creates a stable ecotone (a habitat that exists between two others) able to support biotic replication, including fungus, bacteria, algae, plants, insects, and animals.

This new knowledge has been the subject of thousands of articles, reports, and scientific papers, as well as more than 300 books. There are more than a dozen yearly, quarterly, or monthly publications that feature detailed scientific work on wetlands. This research and writing plays a critical role in educating the public about the health and needs of wetlands. A future challenge is to continue the dialogue on wetlands in multiple venues—including conferences, college-level classes, and publications—ensuring that information is continually shared and new results evaluated.

In the United States, mid-twentieth-century book authors comprised much of the driving force of environmental awareness that resulted in wetland research and protection. Marjory Stoneman Douglas's *The Everglades: River of Grass* (1947) alerted Floridians to a freshwater ecosystem on the verge of complete collapse. Aldo Leopold's *Sand County Almanac* (1949) analyzed the land-use patterns in Sauk County, Wisconsin, and discussed how a lack of conservation ethics had resulted in widespread loss of habitats and wildlife. Rachel Carson's *Silent Spring* (1962) laid out a science-based argument that excessive pesticide use was devastating bird populations, especially in wetlands. All three books awakened a generation to the importance of environmental issues, especially those related to wetlands and other essential ecosystems.

Today's modern interest in wetland ecosystems has resulted in three distinct professional groups that generate numerous technical papers and reports. Each entity has a different approach to its work. Final products vary according to whether they are intended for academic, professional, or lay audiences.

Scientists and Researchers

Many wetland scientists and researchers are based at private or public universities and colleges and generate articles and technical publications intended to be read by their peers. The university researcher often examines the health of one wetland species and its biological features in a particular habitat.

For example, a highly technical paper such as "Seasonal Dynamics in Water Quality and Vegetation Cover in Temporary Pools with Variable Hydroperiods in Kiskunság, Hungary" discusses the seasonal fluctuations of a specific type of wetlands in a specific place. This article was printed in a 2008 issue of *Wetlands,* a journal published by the Society of Wetland Scientists. The lead author, Liesbet Boven, is a researcher at Catholic University in Leuven, Belgium. Another example of a scientific article is "Demographic Responses to Fire of *Spartina Argentinensis* in Temporary Flooded Grassland of Argentina." It was coauthored by Susana R. Feldman and Juan Pablo Lewis, professors at the School of Agriculture, National University of Rosario, Argentina, and published in a 2007 issue of *Wetlands*.

In a given year, hundreds of technical papers such as these contribute to the broader knowledge of wetland resource areas. In addition, more than 450 academic institutions around the globe offer college-level instruction in the professional field of wetland science, including studies at the Institute for Water Education in The Netherlands and a program in wetland resources and the environment at Huazhong Agricultural University in China.

Government Regulators and Professional Wetland Managers

Another primary wetland research group includes government regulators and professional wetland managers. Such professionals may include town conservation administrators, county wetland delineators, state wetland permit reviewers, or federal wetland policy advisers.

This group of researchers uses a multitude of detailed reports to study various areas of concern. For example, the U. S. Army Corps of Engineers has developed a uniform approach to wetland assessments. One of its reports, written in 1995, included "An Approach for Assessing Wetland Functions Using Hydrogeomorphic Classification, Reference Wetlands, and Functional Indices."

The Wetlands Conservation Program, within the South African Department of Environmental Affairs, oversees wetland conservation on a national level. One of their publications, *Biota of South African Wetlands* (1999), documents countrywide wetland species, including 350 plants, 244 fish, 102 amphibians, thirty-six reptiles, 234 birds, and forty-four mammals. This publication disseminates information for the general public about wetland species and plays a role in reducing the piecemeal loss of wetland resources due to lack of knowledge.

Private Organizations

The broadest segment of wetland professional groups, private organizations, focuses on aspects of wetland policy and research. Publications often are used as a centerpiece for an advocacy campaign.

The World Wildlife Fund's report *Orinoco Wetlands in Northeastern Venezuela* (2006) provides an overview of these distinctive freshwater wetlands and emergent threats from water diversion projects and oil drilling efforts. This report educates the broader public on the wetlands but also serves to apply pressure to both regulators and developers, stressing that the resource area is valuable and should not be damaged.

Another private organization, the Korean Wetlands Alliance, developed the *Korean Wetlands Alliance National NGO Wetlands Report* (1999) to highlight South Korea's countrywide wetland issues. This umbrella organization, consisting of environmental groups and individuals, supports educational efforts, scientific research, and campaigns to bring South Korean wetland issues to the public's attention.

Government's Shifting Role in Wetland Conservation

Historically, some governments have managed wetlands by creating reservoirs, building flood control structures, and maintaining inventories of natural resource areas. The most common premise of their actions up until the twentieth century was to utilize these resources for public use and development. If securing drinking water meant digging a canal through a freshwater wetland and building an adjacent holding pond, the government often was relied upon to permit and even perform this work. As the value of wetlands became better understood in the 1960s, many government agencies had to shift their role from developer to protector.

One example tracks the work of the U.S. Army Corps of Engineers, a federal agency that has been working in or near wetlands for over 200 years. The Corps was formed in 1802 as a branch of the military to oversee a number of construction projects. It designed and built military and government buildings, constructed coastal fortifications, dug canals, mapped the country, and inventoried natural areas for a century.

In 1890, the agency's mission was altered by Congress with the passage of the Rivers and Harbors Act. This legislation directed the Corps to become the federal flood control authority, a regulator of dams, a provider of hydroelectric power, and a manager of recreational facilities. It also gave the agency the responsibility of issuing permits to anyone who wanted to dredge, alter, or fill in a wetland or navigable waterway.

In the 1960s, the Corps took on a new and very different charge. As the science of wetlands proved both the immediate and long-term value of wetlands, the public voiced its concern that these resource areas were being destroyed and needed to be protected or preserved for the public benefit.

With passage of the federal Water Pollution Control Act of 1972, the Corps also became the leading environmental regulatory agency, delineating and protecting wetlands and other natural resources. This role involving wetlands is now shared with the U.S. Environmental Protection Agency, as well as with state and local regulatory bodies.

Cooperative Efforts

The task of conserving wetlands is an emergent one for local, regional, and national branches of government around the world. When legislation is signed or a policy adopted that protects a wetland area, a government branch is charged with its implementation. In Canada, 14 percent of the country (490,349 square miles, or 1.2 million square kilometers) consists of wetlands. By the end of the twentieth century, nearly 70 percent of coastal marshes, 50 percent of prairie marshes, and up to 98 percent of urban wetlands had been drained or lost across the country. Canadian conservation groups and the public at large called for major action.

After a three-year public discussion, the national government adopted a Federal Policy on Wetlands Conservation in 1991. This policy requires all government departments to adhere to the no net loss standard, and it sets several other related goals. The legislation addresses various aspects of water systems, habitat preservation, wildlife, fish, and migratory bird management, and threatened or endangered species. Instead of one department performing wetland preservation functions, several larger agencies, each with as many as hundreds of employees, share responsibilities and are held accountable for implementing the stated goals.

A smaller nation such as Madagascar, which has a considerably smaller government, can find it more difficult to effectively enforce its wetland conservation program. With 20 million residents spread across 226,597 square miles (586,886 square kilometers), this island off the southeastern coast of Africa had lost up to one-third of its wetland areas by 1990. In response, the government adopted a law in 1996 that encourages local communities to create resource management associations to protect wildlife habitats.

As part of this program, an area was set aside to protect the Madagascar fish eagle (*Haliaeetus vociferoides*), an endangered species, after extensive habitat loss and predation. The area, managed by a local village, includes wetlands. Only 100 breeding pairs of this rare eagle are thought to remain, so wetlands habitat protection is a central goal to increase the population. Between 1998 and 2007 Madagascar officials also worked closely with the Ramsar Convention staff to protect six additional, separate areas totaling 3,040 square miles (7,874 square kilometers).

Long-Term Approaches

Governments have been seeking more proactive tools to enhance wetland areas. Instead of simply addressing issues when developments, such as building an employment center, parking lot, or access road, are undertaken, cities and towns in many countries have taken a longer-term approach to reduce environmental impacts and degradation.

One example is addressing the problem of storm water runoff from roofs and parking lots. Historically, rain and snowmelt used to be directed off a property through drain systems. However, this potent mix of such contaminants as oil, chemicals, pet waste, garbage, landscape fertilizers, herbicides, and pesticides interacts with water and is damaging to most wetland plants. Therefore, other methods needed to be found for its safe dispersal.

Instead of working country by country, the European Union, which includes twenty-seven countries, used a collaborative, long-term approach, representing 494 million citizens and 1.6 million square miles (4.1 million square kilometers). The European Union passed the Water Framework Directive (WFD) in 2000. The framework outlines a series of environmental objectives to elevate inland and coastal waters to be mostly pollution-free by 2015.

The main goals of the WFD are broad and apply to all rivers, lakes, estuaries, and coastal waters. However, the directive also mandates that groundwater

SPECIFIC GOALS
OF THE WATER FRAMEWORK DIRECTIVE

- Expanding the scope of water protection to all waters (surface and ground).
- Achieving water quality that is almost pollution-free for all waters in the EU by 2015.
- Implementing water management based on an area's river basins.
- Using a combined approach of measurable pollution limits and pollution reduction practices.
- Getting the prices right (mitigation fees must meet the cost of projects).
- Encouraging citizens to get involved more directly.
- Streamlining legislation (seven related laws have been replaced with one).

Source: European Union Environment Program.

should achieve improved water quality and quantity. One objective deals specifi-cally with the handling of storm water runoff. Anyone constructing large prop-erties must install on-site storm water treatment systems. One option is to use constructed wetlands, which temporarily hold and treat water with a variety of plants and bacteria before it is released into adjacent rivers and streams.

Since its implementation, the directive has impacted a wide range of people and activities in the European Union, including water consumers, recreational users of natural resources, and the agriculture, industry, and business sectors. Compliance with the directive will help prevent further deterioration in the qual-ity of inland and coastal waters and promote sustainable water consumption.

Commercial and Industrial Long-Term Planning

One wetland protection strategy in both the public and private sectors involves better planning at construction sites to reduce environmental and wetland im-pacts. With land costs escalating, developers often seek cheaper land near road systems. This has meant growth in rural areas away from populations, causing immediate impacts on pristine environments. Developed in response to sprawl in rural areas, a movement called "smart growth" has pushed for better community planning to cluster employment and residential centers near one another.

The Vermont Forum on Sprawl, a nonprofit organization based in Burlington, Vermont, works to protect the rural landscape of the Green Moun-tains. In 2003, the forum released a document titled "New Models for Commercial and Industrial Development." Developed in collaboration with a statewide business group, the Vermont Business Roundtable, the report offers a series of suggestions to improve land use and environmental protection at the same time.

Other communities in the United States, such as Boulder County, Colorado, have worked to control growth and protect the environment by creating an open space band, or greenbelt, around the city center. In the case of the city of Boulder, the goal is to slow and target growth and reduce wetland degradation outside the heart of the community.

Beginning in 1959, limits were imposed on locations where city water lines could be built, and such limits consequently controlled growth. In 1967, a tax for purchasing open space to create this protective greenbelt was added, with additional taxes levied in 1989. By 2007, the county had protected up to 70,000 acres (23,328 hectares) of open space. Although houses exist within the greenbelt, Boulder residents enjoy a 6- to 8-mile (9.7- to 12.9-kilometer) band of mostly open space surrounding the city center, including 1,207 acres (489 hectares) of wetlands.

Long-term planning allows both human development and advanced wetland protection. Creative and cost-effective models that mitigate pollution or create on-site wetlands to treat storm water have proven successful in protecting adjacent wetland resources. Such plans provide tangible solutions for resourceful and eco-conscious communities.

Selected Web Sites

Boulder County, Colorado, Parks & Open Space: http://www.co.boulder.co.us/openspace/.

European Union Water Framework Directive: http://ec.europa.eu/environment/water/water-framework/.

Population-Environment Balance: htpp://www.balance.org.

Smart Growth Vermont: htpp://www.vtsprawl.org.

U.S. Environmental Protection Agency: http://www.epa.gov.

U.S. Fish and Wildlife Service, North American Waterfowl Management Plan: http://www.fws.gov/birdhabitat/NAWMP/.

Further Reading

Agricultural Conservation and Wetlands. Washington, DC: U.S. General Accounting Office, 2003.

Boulder County Open Space Department. "Open Space Presentation 1975 Through 2005." Boulder, CO: Boulder County Government, 2006.

Carson, Rachel. *Silent Spring.* 1962. New York: Houghton Mifflin, 2002.

Conserving America's Wetlands 2007. Washington, DC: White House Council on Environmental Quality, 2007.

Douglas, Marjory Stoneman. *Everglades: River of Grass.* 1947. Sarasota, FL: Pineapple, 2007.

European Union Water Framework Directive. Brussels, Belgium: European Union, 2006.

Leopold, Aldo. *Sand County Almanac.* 1949. New York: Oxford University Press, 2001.

New Models for Commercial and Industrial Development. Burlington, VT: Vermont Forum on Sprawl, 2003.

North American Waterfowl Management Plan: Continental Progress Assessment, 2005. Washington, DC: U.S. Fish and Wildlife Service, 2005.

Sibbing, Julie. *Nowhere Near No-Net-Loss.* Washington, DC: National Wildlife Federation, 2005.

Status and Trends of Wetlands in the Conterminous United States, 1998 to 2004. Washington, DC: U.S. Fish and Wildlife Service, 2006.

U.S. Library of Congress. *Wetland Issues.* Washington, DC: Congressional Research Service, 2003.

12 A Wetland's Value

Wetlands are unique, biologically productive areas that historically have been misrepresented and undervalued. Compared to many of the world's other natural features, such as mountains and forests, wetlands have not received similar recognition as environmentally significant resource areas. As discussed throughout this book, most wetlands have been treaded upon, dumped into, filled in, and otherwise degraded for years. Only in the latter part of the twentieth century did a respect for these distinctive ecosystems emerge.

In order to protect the world's estimated remaining 4.9 million square miles (12.7 million square kilometers) of wetlands, a multifaceted approach must be implemented in the twenty-first century. Tactics include increasing the global awareness of the value of wetlands, conducting more thorough and uniform worldwide wetland inventories and assessments, improving economic policies so that they take into consideration the protection and conservation of wetlands, balancing water use habits so that they do not harm wetlands, and addressing the root causes of climate change.

A New Consciousness

The year 1983 brought a major turning point for wetlands. The wetland scientist Paul Adamus, working for the Center for Natural Areas, at the Washington, D.C.–based Smithsonian Institution, produced a report that outlined numerous benefits provided by wetlands. These benefits included storing fertilizers loaded with nitrates and phosphates, purifying sewage-laden water, anchoring storm-battered shorelines, and reducing the effects of floods. Adamus also created a wetlands function assessment for the nonscientist to use in evaluating wetland features.

Adamus's assessment did more than help evaluate valuable wetland functions. It also proved, with basic analytical tools, that wetlands are essential to human health and safety. His report was accepted in major circles of industry and by many governments. No longer were wetlands considered merely obstructions to building a new highway or an office complex. Protecting them had become an essential aspect of protecting both the broader environment and, ultimately, the well-being of humanity.

At about the same time, economists, government officials, and industry executives began to recognize the economic value of wetlands. In a 1999 article in the journal *Nature,* University of Maryland researcher Robert Costanza and a dozen of his colleagues from around the world developed models to estimate the monetary value of various environmental functions.

A wetland restoration in Marion, Virginia, shows the first stage of the project, where tree saplings were placed within piping that functions as a protective layer to help the trees resist disease such as fungus and limit wildlife damage through browsing. The site work performed here also included closing a drainage structure, installing a livestock crossing and fencing to keep cattle out of the wetland, and planting wetland vegetation. Once the work was completed, the habitat was suitable for other wetland plant and animal species to become established. (Jeff Vanuga/U.S. Department of Agriculture, Natural Resources Conservation Service)

They estimated a value produced from seventeen natural systems—atmosphere, water supply, wetlands, and so on—on Earth: $54 trillion per year. Wetland systems made up $15.5 trillion of that annual amount, up to 30 percent of the total value of ecosystem services. Even though wetlands cover just about 10 percent of Earth's surface, they provide almost a third of such services, including water supply and filtration, carbon sequestering, oxygen production, erosion protection, and flood control.

Although individual countries around the world have recognized the value of wetlands and have taken bold steps to catalogue, conserve, and protect ecosystems within their boundaries, the loss of wetlands continues. Global losses of wetlands in the nineteenth and twentieth centuries exceed half of what was in existence around 2000 B.C.E., a loss of more than 5 million square miles (13 million square kilometers), or half the landmass of the entire African continent.

The reduction in the number of planetary wetlands has resulted in a spectrum of costly environmental impacts. These include high salinity in the Baltic Sea, loss of migrating birds in subarctic Canada, loss of freshwater fish in China, reduced water quality in Great Britain, reduced biodiversity in South America, and increased flooding in the United States.

Changing Wetland Inventory and Assessment

In 1996, Wetlands International produced the report "A Global Overview of Wetlands Loss and Degradation," which described steep wetland losses across the planet. Their surveys found that 13 percent of China's wetlands have been eliminated, 35 percent have been lost in Mexico, 80 percent lost in Colombia, 90 percent in New Zealand, and nearly 100 percent in Israel.

Having an accurate inventory of wetlands is critical to understanding these ecosystems and responding to their preservation and restoration. However, the 1996 report concluded by saying,

1. There is a lack of information about loss and degradation in most countries; much of the information that does exist cannot be compared.

2. A global overview indicates that massive historical losses of wetlands have occurred worldwide, much of this prior to the launch of the Ramsar Convention. There are wide variations between regions, between wetland types, and over time.

3. The majority of the remaining wetlands are degraded, or under threat of degradation. The intensity of these problems is closely related to the intensity of human activity in and around the wetland.

4. The loss and degradation of wetlands has severe economic consequences, and removes opportunities for sustainable development. Restoration and rehabilitation measures are very expensive, and unlikely to restore full natural functions.

5. We [Wetlands International] are not in a position to measure the global wetland resource baseline, nor to monitor the success of national and international programmes, including the Ramsar Convention.

6. Information on the loss and degradation of wetlands is essential to influence policy, through public awareness.

Since the 1980s, wetland mapping has shifted from ground-based to space-based surveys, which provide a more accurate inventory. Developments in space-based wetland mapping bring researchers higher resolution, and therefore more accurate, images that display multiple variables—not just area and size, but also vegetation type and even water temperatures.

Captured by orbiting satellites, such images can be rephotographed at intervals to monitor the ongoing status of the sites. No longer are aerial pictures from a plane and weeks of time-consuming fieldwork the staple of assessing a wetland. Instead, images are taken and delivered within a few minutes. And for the first time, many of these images have been made available to the public through the Internet.

Advanced mapping with updated data is an essential component to better understanding wetland habitats. The International Water Management Institute (IWMI), a scientific research organization based in Sri Lanka, established a Global Wetland Inventory and Mapping Program in 2007 to set up uniform standards for more thorough inventories. Working with Ramsar and leading wetland researchers, the institute's goals include establishing mapping needs and developing a network of local, regional, state, and federal expertise and capabilities.

One project in 2007 included wetlands mapping in the areas of Sri Lanka, India, Thailand, and Indonesia, where a December 26, 2006, undersea earthquake had caused a tsunami that battered the shoreline and took up to 300,000 lives. The IWMI, collaborating with other wetlands organizations, developed a rapid assessment of the affected areas with before and after satellite imagery. This information was used to help planners adjust resettlement efforts to avoid wetland resource and flood-prone areas. The map service that was developed is readily accessible on the Internet for regional government partners to utilize.

In 2009, the U.S. Department of the Interior, which oversees all national wetland inventories, announced the adoption of a Wetlands Mapping Standard to improve the consistency of federally funded satellite-generated digital maps.

Improving Economic Policies

Especially in developing countries, a major historic cause of wetland loss has been the construction of infrastructure projects—roads, dams, airports, factories, other large buildings, and so on. Almost all of these projects have relied on international financial lending institutions for funding.

This financial field is led by two organizations, The World Bank and the International Monetary Fund (IMF); both were formed shortly after World War II and are based in Washington, D.C. These two organizations loan money for large infrastructure projects and other economic development efforts worldwide. Collectively, they have loaned several trillion dollars since the mid-twentieth century. The bulk of these loans has resulted in substantial economic and social progress for the borrowing countries.

Such infrastructure improvements, however, often have come at the cost of wetland habitats. Neither The World Bank nor the International Money Fund has adopted any goals regarding halting wetland losses. In the last decade of the twentieth century, however, both have modified their review processes. Rather than approving a project solely on its economic merits, they now take into consideration the full range of a country's social, political, cultural, and environmental issues and consider related impacts.

The World Bank has supported almost 500 large dams in ninety-two countries, resulting in sizable wetland losses and human population displacements. After criticism from environmental organizations, as well as borrowing countries, The World Bank adopted internal review processes in 1990 that seek to reduce impacts on the natural environment. In 1999, The World Bank began publishing *The Little Green Data Book* annually to highlight environmental problems; the 2008 version focuses on climate change. The book provides detailed facts, country by country, on agricultural output, emissions, pollution, sanitation, and water use issues.

The International Monetary Fund followed a similar path in 1998, recognizing that "severe environmental degradation can affect a country's macro-economic performance over the long run." A statement from the International Monetary Fund expressed the relationship between economic activities and the natural environment:

> Economic activities affect, and are affected by, the natural environment in diverse and complex ways, many of which have only recently become the subject of systematic analysis. Meanwhile, public concern about environmental conditions and the impact of economic policies on the environment has mounted. The IMF Board has concluded that IMF staff

should develop a greater understanding of the interplay between economic policies, economic activity, and environmental change. This would help to avoid the possibility that the IMF might recommend policies that could have undesirable environmental consequences, while ensuring that the thrust of its actions—promoting sustainable growth and reducing poverty—also helps mitigate environmental concerns.

Balancing Water Control Practices and Wetlands

Human water control has caused significant damage to wetlands over time. Such systems began centuries ago with hand-dug, gravity-fed irrigation ditches, which were followed by man-made ponds, dikes, and reservoirs, and eventually dams. Grander changes to hydrological flow often resulted in multiple problems for natural systems, causing erosion, drought, or flooding.

The Millennium Ecosystem Assessment, performed by the Washington, D.C.–based World Resources Institute in 2005, examined 227 river basins around the world. It found that 37 percent of rivers suffered from fragmentation and impaired flows. The study revealed that there are 1,856 types of amphibians, of which 964 live year-round in water or wetlands. Up to 33 percent are threatened with extinction. At the same time, 23 percent of mammal species and 12 percent of bird species are under threat.

The Mississippi River displays major water modification failures, particularly in the area where it meets the Gulf of Mexico. The lower reaches of the river have been straightened to ease shipping passage. Although this has helped barge and boat transport, increased currents also carry more sediment down river, resulting in 120 million tons of sediment being washed directly into the deep waters of the Gulf of Mexico each year.

At the same time, the adjacent wetlands in Louisiana and Mississippi have been shrinking due to reduced inflows of sediment and water. Since 1930, the southern delta has lost up to 1.2 million acres (485,623 square hectares) of wetlands—an area roughly the size of the state of Delaware. Lost wetlands have meant widespread coastal flooding and land erosion.

In 2007, scientists and state and federal policymakers began a dialogue about how to redirect the river into wetlands to restore these ecosystems. One proposal that is being evaluated is to rebuild these wetlands by closing some shipping channels so that sediment can build up and allow plant communities to re-establish.

Another noteworthy water project that eliminated wetlands is the Jordan River diversion, which runs between the Hashemite Kingdom of Jordan and the West Bank in the Middle East. Beginning in 1964, Israel and Jordan's modifications for agricultural irrigation and public drinking water turned the river into a trickle. The Jordan River historically drained into the Dead Sea; however, without this freshwater flow, the salt lake has sunk from 1,295 feet (395 meters) below sea level in 1970 to 1,371 feet (418 meters) below sea level in 2006, and its salinity now ranges from 26 to 35 percent (ocean water averages 3.5 percent).

As of 2010, the wetlands that lined the Jordan River and the Dead Sea are almost all gone. Discussions on how to restore the Dead Sea have focused on efforts to increase freshwater inflow from the Jordan River. Due to recent regional military Arab-Israeli conflicts, no agreements have yet been reached.

Around the globe, the construction of massive dams has inflicted extensive damage to wetlands by reducing water flows. Wetlands cannot thrive in dam-influenced conditions such as rapidly changing water levels with little sediment in the water flow.

The Columbia River begins in western Canada and crosses into the United States, traveling between Washington and Oregon during its 1,243-mile (2,000-kilometer) journey to the Pacific Ocean. During the twentieth century,

This fish ladder was installed at the Bonneville Dam on the Columbia River between the states of Washington and Oregon to assist native salmon and steelhead trout in swimming upstream to their spawning grounds. Unfortunately, this and similar measures have not done enough to help save still declining fish populations in the Pacific Northwest. *(Tim Matsui/Getty Images)*

HYDROELECTRIC DAMS ON THE COLUMBIA RIVER

Dam	Location	Capacity (Megawatts)
Keenleyside	Canada	185
Rock Island	Washington State	660
Wells	Washington State	840
Priest Rapids	Washington State	955
Mcnary	Between Oregon and Washington State	980
Wanapum	Washington State	1,038
Bonneville	Between Oregon and Washington State	1,050
Rocky Reach	Washington State	1,287
The Dalles	Between Oregon and Washington State	1,780
Mica	Canada	1,805
Revelstoke	Canada	1,980
John Day	Between Oregon and Washington State	2,160
Chief Joseph	Washington State	2,620
Grand Coulee	Washington State	6,809
	Total Generating Capacity:	24,149

Source: U.S. Army Corps of Engineers, 2003.

fourteen hydroelectric dams were built along the river, creating an impressive 24,149 megawatts of electricity on a given day and altering the flow and wetland habitats along its length.

As a result of these changes, species such as Chinook salmon (*Oncorhynchus tshawytscha*), which once thrived in the Columbia, have barely survived, despite the installation of fish ladders designed to allow the salmon to travel upstream to spawn. In 2006, a federal judge declared that the federal government is not doing enough to protect the endangered species in the Columbia River region. The court issued a ruling stating that the government must intensify its efforts, which may include dam removals. The Marmot Dam, located on Sandy River—a tributary to the Columbia—was the first to be removed in 2007.

Despite such actions being taken in the United States and other countries, there were 45,000 dams in existence worldwide and 1,600 new dams under construction in 2008. Responding to environmental damage caused by such structures, the United Nation's World Commission on Dams released a report titled *Dam and Development: A New Framework for Decision Making* in 2000. This document drew attention to how dams impact human rights, alter river flows, damage wetlands, and lower fish populations.

Addressing Climate Change

Climate change poses one of the most serious threats to wetlands across the planet. In 2007, the International Panel on Climate Change, made up of members of the United Nations and the World Meteorological Organization, released the largest study to date on global warming, amassing the scientific work of 600 authors from forty countries. The *Fourth Assessment on Climate Change 2007* found that "Global atmospheric concentrations of carbon dioxide, ethane, and nitrous oxide have increased markedly as a result of human activities since 1750."

The pre-industrial measurement of carbon dioxide was approximately 280 parts per million. In 2008, this amount climbed to 383 parts per million, far exceeding the highest level in the last 650,000 years. As of 2009, this level was continuing to increase by roughly 2 parts per million per year.

The study revealed that greenhouse gas accumulation has increased planetary temperatures, elevated water vapor rates, raised ocean temperatures, melted mountain and glacier snow cover, and elevated sea levels (.07 inches, or 1.8 millimeters, per year for the past century) from melting polar ice caps. By 2025, sea levels could be 3 feet (1 meter) higher than in 2007. Between 1995 and 2007, temperatures exceeded the warmest in recorded history.

The report outlined additional impacts on wetlands, including ozone depletion in the upper atmosphere, worsening air quality due to increased amounts of carbon dioxide, methane, and aerosols, more frequent floods and droughts as weather patterns fluctuate, and a loss in habitat and biodiversity of animal species. These impacts are primarily the result of hydrological system changes such as water temperature increases, rising sea levels, and more intense storm systems, floods, and droughts.

The report summarized that while some wetland plants will grow faster with hotter weather, more carbon dioxide, increased precipitation, and inflow of water, many wetlands will be severely damaged. Coastal marshes will be submerged underwater, estuaries will experience salinity contamination from ocean inundation upriver, and many plant and animal species will not be able to adapt to the environmental changes, with the result that some species will become extinct.

A segment of the 2007 report released by the International Panel on Climate Change outlined mitigation efforts to stabilize greenhouse gases. Drafted by 400 scientists and experts from 120 countries, the document presents a number of short-term (through 2030) and long-term (2030 to 2050) changes to sectors of the worldwide economy concerned with energy, transportation, industry, agriculture, forestry, and waste.

These measures include a reduction of point and non-point source pollution (factories versus cars), better technology to reduce reliance on carbon-based fuel sources, and better use of mass transportation systems. World carbon dioxide emissions from human sources were estimated at 29 billion tons in 2006. This number is forecasted to grow to 40 billion tons by 2030. The report concluded that if sufficient global mitigation efforts are undertaken by 2030, up to 6 billion tons of carbon dioxide per year could be eliminated from the atmosphere at a cost of 5 percent or less of the world's gross domestic product.

One of the most challenging issues raised by the IPCC regarding climate change is human behavior. In order to lower emissions, many lifestyle changes will have to be adopted, including altering daily habits to consume less energy and resources, as well as increasing energy efficiency.

Wetlands, as reviewed in this book, appear across the planet in a variety of types and weather climates. Their formation often is a result of natural changes in the landscape: an earthquake leaving behind a depression; a glacier carving a basin and depositing debris; or a riverbed dug out through the centuries of water flow.

In a geologic timescale, wetlands are formed abruptly and their existence is but temporary. After a few thousand years, all wetlands come to an eventual end by forces similar to those that created them: An erupting volcano covers the land with fresh lava; the wetlands fill in from layers of decaying vegetation and a forest emerges; their water source is rerouted; or the climate weather pattern changes, and they cannot survive.

In the last century, the scientific view of these habitats has gone from one of useless and dreaded wastelands to biologically rich and beneficial environmental systems. This new appreciation of the value and functions of wetlands has changed many outlooks and resulted in a movement to protect their uniqueness, planet-wide.

Wetlands now are seen as a cradle for wildlife and plant communities. They filter freshwater for public water supplies. They protect homes from flooding. They even remove toxic pollution from waters and slowly release it in a non-toxic form back into the environment.

But with a growing population and the related ever-increasing consumption of land, water, and natural resources, wetlands are under threat and face an uncertain future. For wetlands to thrive, people in every community and every culture must understand their importance as well as manage them wisely for the long term.

In 1869, the naturalist John Muir was living in the Yosemite region of central California when he remarked on how the environment is interconnected: "When we try to pick out anything by itself, we find it hitched to everything else in the universe." Ultimately, humans and wetlands need each other for a healthy and sustainable future.

Selected Web Sites

Intergovernmental Panel on Climate Change: http://www.ipcc.ch.

International Water Management Institute: http://www.iwmi.cgiar.org.

Ramsar Convention on Wetlands: http://www.ramsar.org.

U.S. Army Corps of Engineers Wetland Evaluation Technique: http://el.erdc.usace.army.mil/emrrp/emris/emrishelp6/wetland_evaluation_technique_tools.htm.

United Nations Framework Convention on Climate Change: http://www.unfccc.int.

The World Bank: http://go.worldbank.org.

Further Reading

Finlayson, Max, et al. *Global Wetland Inventory and Mapping*. Colombo, Sri Lanka: International Water Management Institute, 2006.

Mitsch, William, James G. Gosselink, Li Zhang, and Christopher J. Anderson. *Wetland Ecosystems*. Hoboken, NJ: John Wiley and Sons, 2009.

Muir, John. *My First Summer in the Sierras*. 1911. New York: Penguin, 1997.

Nivet, Chris. *A Review of Wetland Inventory Information*. Gelderland Province, The Netherlands: Wetlands International, 2002.

Sever, Megan. "Restoring the River." *Geotimes,* Publication of the American Geological Institute, August 2007.

United Nations. *State of the World Population 2006*. New York: United Nations Population Fund, 2006.

United Nations and the World Meteorological Organization. *Climate Change 2007: The Physical Science Basis*. Geneva, Switzerland: Intergovernmental Panel on Climate Change, 2007.

The World Bank. *Little Green Data Book 2007*. Washington, DC: World Bank, 2007.

Acid rain. Rain or other precipitation that is unusually acidic. It is the result of emissions of carbon, nitrogen, and sulfur (typically from industry), which react with water to form acids. Acid rain causes harm to animals, plants, soils, and structures.

Algae. A diverse group of photosynthetic, single-cell and multicellular aquatic organisms. Most algae live at or near the surface of wetlands, freshwater bodies, or oceans, and are consumed by species such as copepods. There are approximately 15,000 different species of algae worldwide.

Anaerobic. Organisms that are able to live with little or no oxygen.

Aquifer. An underground layer of permeable rock, gravel, soil, or sand from which groundwater can be extracted.

Atmosphere. The mixture of gases surrounding the Earth. By volume, it consists of about 78.08 percent nitrogen, 20.95 percent oxygen, 0.93 percent argon, 0.036 percent carbon dioxide, and trace amounts of other gases, including helium, hydrogen, methane, and ozone.

Bacteria. Simple, single-celled microorganisms that live in soil, water, organic matter, and the bodies of plants and animals. Some bacteria are pathogenic—that is, responsible for causing infectious diseases.

Biodiversity. Biological diversity, indicated by the variety of living organisms and ecosystems in which they live.

Biomass. The total weight of all living organisms in a defined community at one time.

Biome. A regional ecosystem that is characterized by a particular climate and biological community.

Biosolids. Nutrient-rich by-products of sewage sludge, or the residue created by sewage treatment.

Biosphere. The ecological system made up of all living organisms on Earth.

Bog. An enclosed wetland that is fed primarily by precipitation and characterized by acidic water and low levels of nutrients. Bogs contain peat, an accumulation of decayed plant matter.

Brackish. A mixture of freshwater and salt water.

Carbon dioxide (CO_2). A gas that is found naturally in the atmosphere at a concentration of 0.036 percent. It is fundamental to life, required for respiration and photosynthesis.

Carbon neutral. A state in which no carbon is released into the environment, achieved through controlling the emission and absorption of carbon.

Carbon sink. A natural or man-made reservoir or habitat that can store carbon for long periods of time (such as wetlands, forests, or oceans).

Climate change. Global variation in the Earth's climate over time. A recent phenomenon (measured over the last two centuries), it is attributable largely to human atmospheric pollution. Climate change results in temperature increases and other shifts in weather patterns, severe droughts and floods, rising sea levels, and biotic changes (often causing the loss of species in an area).

Conservation. The protection, preservation, management, or restoration of natural resources, plants, and wildlife.

Decomposition. The process by which organic matter is broken down by dynamic forces, such as weather, water, and microbes.

Dilution method. The dumping of waste into water bodies or groundwater wells, where it is diluted by the movement of water and, theoretically, made less potent.

Discharge. The release of untreated waste into waterways, often following excessive precipitation that exceeds the capacity of a sewer system or waste processing facility.

Ecosystem. The interaction of a biological community and its environment.

Effluent. The outflow of water from a wastewater treatment plant or septic tank.

Endangered (and threatened) species. A species that is in danger of extinction because the total population is insufficient to reproduce enough offspring to ensure its survival. A threatened species exhibits declining or dangerously low population but still has enough members to maintain or increase numbers.

Endemic. A plant or animal that is native to and occupies a limited geographic area.

Environment. External conditions that affect an organism or community.

Erosion. The removal of materials from a location as a result of wind or water currents.

Eutrophication. Algae blooms in aquatic ecosystems that are caused by excessive concentrations of organic and inorganic nutrients, including garden and lawn fertilizers and sewage system discharges. These blooms reduce dissolved oxygen in the water when dead plant material decomposes, causing other organisms, such as fish and crabs, to die.

Fen. A type of wetland that is fed by groundwater or surface water; typically, it is less acidic than a bog.

Floodplains. Low lying, flood-prone land areas that are adjacent to rivers and other waterways.

Greenhouse effect. A warming of the Earth's atmosphere caused by the presence of heat-trapping gases in the atmosphere—primarily carbon dioxide, nitrous oxide, ozone, water vapor, and methane—mimicking the effect of a greenhouse.

Groundwater. Water below the Earth's surface.

Habitat. An area in which a particular plant or animal can live, grow, and reproduce naturally.

Hazardous waste. Industrial and household chemicals and other wastes that are highly toxic to humans and the environment.

Herbicides. Chemicals that are used to kill or inhibit the growth of plants. Selective herbicides kill a specific type of plant, while nonselective herbicides kill all plants.

Hydrologic cycle. The continuous movement of water as a result of evaporation, precipitation, and groundwater or surface water flows.

Hydrology. The science of the movement and properties of water both above ground and underground.

Inorganic chemicals. Mineral-based compounds that do not contain carbon among their principal elements (such as acids, metals, minerals, and salts).

Insecticides. Chemicals used to kill insects that are harmful to plant and animal communities.

Mangrove. A type of wetland found in both freshwater and salt water, characterized by trees with long, spidery roots that grow in and above the water.

Marsh. A type of wetland found in both freshwater and salt water that has a high water table. The vegetation in a marsh is dominated by grasses.

Nitrates. A form of naturally occurring nitrogen that is found in fertilizers, human waste, and landfills and can cause eutrophication in wetlands and open water.

Non-point source. A source of pollution that comes from a broad area (such as car and truck emissions) rather than a single point of origin (known as a point source).

Nutrients. Chemicals that are necessary for organic growth and reproduction. For example, the primary plant nutrients are nitrogen, phosphorus, and potassium.

Organic chemicals. A large family of carbon-based chemicals, such as methane and vitamin B. By comparison, inorganic chemicals often are mineral-based, such as chloride and sodium.

pH. A measurement of the acidity or alkalinity of a solution, referring to the potential (p) of the hydrogen (H) ion concentration. The pH scale ranges from 0 to 14; acidic substances have lower pH values, while alkaline or basic substances have higher values.

Phosphorus. An element in the nitrogen family that, in high concentrations, can cause eutrophication in a body of water.

Point source. A source of pollution that originates from a single point, such as the discharge end of a pipe or a power plant.

Prairie pothole. A type of wetland that is characterized by clustered depressions in the ground formed by glacial activity. These wetlands are common in the inland plains of the United States and Canada.

Quaking bog. A wetland in which floating vegetation covers a lake's surface.

Raised bog. A wetland with accumulating peat growth that creates a central dome of vegetation above the water level. This dome relies on precipitation for nourishment.

Storm water runoff. The potent mix of nutrients, oils, dirt, and trash that is flushed from the land by rain, ending up in wetlands, rivers, streams, lakes, oceans, and groundwater.

Succession. Changes in the structure and composition of an ecological community. Succession is driven by the immigration of new species and the competitive struggle among species for nutrients and space.

Swamp. A type of wetland that has year-round water coverage. Vegetation may include shrubs, mangroves, or other trees and forest vegetation that have adapted to the hydrologic conditions.

Taxa. The classification of organisms in an ordered, hierarchical system that indicates their natural relationships. The taxa system consists of the following categories: kingdom, phylum, class, order, family, genus, and species.

Thermal pollution. The discharge of heated or cooled water into a lake, river, stream, or other body of water, resulting in a change in ambient water temperature that is harmful to plants and animals. Such pollution is caused by the disposal of industrial wastewater or water from the cooling towers of nuclear power plants.

Total maximum daily load (TMDL). The quantity of chemicals (such as nitrogen and phosphorus) that can be discharged into a waterway from all recognized sources (such as businesses, farms, septic systems, and street runoff) while still maintaining applicable water quality standards.

Virus. Microorganisms (approximately 10 to 100 times smaller than bacteria) that cause infectious diseases such as influenza and smallpox. Viruses are parasites in that they cannot replicate outside the cells of the host organism.

Water (H_2O). A tasteless, odorless liquid formed by two parts of hydrogen and one part of oxygen.

Water table. The level at which water is maintained in a particular ecosystem.

Watershed. A portion of land where all of the water runoff drains into the same body of water; also called a drainage basin.

Wetland. A low-lying area where a high level of saturation by water provides a habitat that is critical to plant and animal life.

For additional Web Sites on more specific topics, please see the Web Site listings in individual chapters.

Alaska Department of Fish and Game Wildlife Conservation: http://www.wildlife.alaska.gov.

Central Asia Regional Water Information Base Project, The Aral Sea Basin: http://www.cawater-info.net/aral/index_e.htm.

Chinese University Report on Poyang Lake: http://www.iseis.cuhk.edu.hk/yuenyuen/project/poyang/poyang.htm.

Danube Delta Biosphere Reserve Agency. http://www.ddbra.ro/en.

Danube Delta National Institute for Research and Development: http://www.indd.tim.ro.

Ducks Unlimited: http://www.ducks.org.

European Commission, Environment: http://ec.europa.eu/environment/index_en.htm.

Everglades National Park Site: http://www.nps.gov/ever.

Food and Agriculture Organization of the United Nations: http://www.fao.org.

Friends of the Everglades: http://www.everglades.org.

Intergovernmental Panel on Climate Change: http://www.ipcc.ch.

International Commission for the Protection of the Danube River: http://www.icpdr.org.

International Water Management Institute: http://www.iwmi.cgiar.org.

Izembek National Wildlife Refuge: http://izembek.fws.gov/.

LakeNet, World Lakes Network: htpp://www.worldlakes.org.

National Geographic Pantanal Profile: http://www.nationalgeographic.com/wildworld/profiles/terrestrial/nt/nt0907.html.

National Oceanic and Atmospheric Administration: www.noaa.gov.

National Wetland Trust of New Zealand: http://www.wetlandtrust.org.nz.

New Zealand Department of Conservation: http://www.doc.govt.nz.

Ramsar Convention on Wetlands: http://www.ramsar.org.

Science Museum of China, Lake Museum: http://www.kepu.com.cn/english/lake.

Society of Wetland Scientists: http://www.sws.org.

State of Florida Everglades Forever Site: http://www.dep.state.fl.us/evergladesforever.

U.S. Environmental Protection Agency: http://www.epa.gov.

U.S Fish and Wildlife Service: http://www.fws.gov.

U.S. Geological Survey: http://www.usgs.gov.

United Nations Environment Programme: http://www.unep.or.jp.

United Nations Framework Convention on Climate Change: http://www.unfccc. int.

Wetlands Care Australia: http://www.wetlandcare.com.au.

Wetlands International: http://www.wetlands.org.

Wildfowl and Wetlands Trust (Great Britain): http://www.wwt.org.uk.

World Wildlife Fund: http://www.worldwildlife.org.

Agricultural Conservation and Wetlands. Washington, DC: U.S. General Accounting Office, 2003.

Batzer, Darold, ed. *Ecology of Freshwater and Estuarine Wetlands.* Berkeley: University of California Press, 2007.

Biebighauser, Thomas. *Wetland Drainage, Restoration, and Repair.* Lexington: University Press of Kentucky, 2007.

Bobbink, Roland, ed. *Wetlands: Functioning, Biodiversity Conservation, and Restoration.* New York: Springer, 2006.

Boulder County Open Space Department. "Open Space Presentation 1975 Through 2005." Boulder, CO: Boulder County Government, 2006.

Carson, Rachel. *Silent Spring.* 1962. New York: Houghton Mifflin, 2002.

Carter, W. Hodding. *Stolen Water: Saving the Everglades from Its Friends, Foes, and Florida.* New York: Atria, 2004.

Chen, S. *Modeling the Impacts of Land Use on Sediment Load in Wetlands of the Poyang Lake Basin.* St. Joseph, MI: American Society of Agricultural and Biological Engineers, 2006.

Chinese University of Hong Kong. *Monitoring the Dynamic Changes of Poyang Lake Wetlands Through Remote Sensing.* Shatin, Hong Kong: Institute of Space and Earth Information Science, 2005.

Conserving America's Wetlands 2007. Washington, DC: White House Council on Environmental Quality, 2007.

Cronk, Julie. *Wetland Plants: Biology and Ecology.* Boca Raton, FL: CRC, 2001.

Datong, Ning. *An Assessment of the Economic Losses Resulting From Various Forms of Environmental Degradation in China.* Beijing: China Environmental Sciences Press, 2001.

Douglas, Marjory Stoneman. *The Everglades: River of Grass.* 1947. Sarasota, FL: Pineapple, 2007.

Dugan, Patrick. *Guide to Wetlands.* Buffalo, NY: Firefly, 2005.

Dukhovny, V.A. *The Aral Sea: Past, Present, and Future.* Tashkent, Uzbekistan: Interstate Commission for Water Coordination, 2008.

Environment Waikato Association. *Restoring Waikato's Indigenous Biodiversity.* Waikato, New Zealand: Waikato Biodiversity Forum, 2006.

European Union Water Framework Directive. Brussels, Belgium: European Union, 2006.

Ferguson, Rob. The Devil and the Disappearing Sea. Vancouver, Canada: Raincoast, 2003.

Finlayson, Max, et al. *Global Wetland Inventory and Mapping.* Colombo, Sri Lanka: International Water Management Institute, 2006.

Fraser, Lauchlan, and Paul A. Keddy, eds. *The World's Largest Wetlands: Ecology and Conservation.* Cambridge, UK: Cambridge University Press, 2005.

Gastescu, Petre. *Danube Delta: A Biosphere Reserve.* Constanta, Romania: Dobrogea Editing House, 2006.

Gilman, Kevin. *Hydrology and Wetland Conservation.* New York: John Wiley and Sons, 2004.

Grunwald, Michael. *The Swamp: The Everglades, Florida, and Politics of Paradise.* New York: Simon and Schuster, 2006.

Hanganu, J. *Vegetation of the Danube Delta Biosphere Reserve.* Bucharest, Romania: Danube Delta National Institute, 2002.

Hunt, Janet. *Wetlands of New Zealand.* New York: Random House, 2007.

Jansjy, Libor. *The Danube: Environmental Monitoring of An International River.* New York: United Nations University Press, 2004.

Leopold, Aldo. *Sand County Almanac.* 1949. New York: Oxford University Press, 2001.

Marx, Trish. *Everglades Forever: Restoring America's Great Wetland.* New York: Lee and Low, 2004.

Michlin, Philip. "Water in the Aral Sea Basin of Central Asia: Cause of Conflict or Cooperation?" Eurasian Geography and Economics 43:7 (2002): 505–528.

Mitsch, William, and James G. Gosselink. *Wetlands.* Hoboken, NJ: John Wiley and Sons, 2007.

Mitsch, William, James G. Gosselink, Li Zhang, and Christopher J. Anderson. *Wetland Ecosystems.* Hoboken, NJ: John Wiley and Sons, 2009.

Mittermeier, Russell. *Pantanal: South America's Wetland Jewel.* Arlington, VA: Conservation International, 2005.

Moon, Geoff. *New Zealand Wetland Birds and Their World.* French's Forest, Australia: New Holland Books, 2009.

Moore, Peter. *Wetlands.* New York: Facts on File, 2001.

Morimoto, Yukihiro. "The Pelican Scenario for Nature Restoration of the Aral Sea Wetland Ecosystems." Landscape and Ecological Engineering, Tokyo, Japan, 2005.

Muir, John. *My First Summer in the Sierras.* 1911. New York: Penguin, 1997.

Murphy, Michael. "A Comparison of Fish Assemblages in Eelgrass and Adjacent Sub-Tidal Habitats Near Craig, Alaska." *Alaska Fishery Research Bulletin,* Volume 7, 2000.

New Models for Commercial and Industrial Development. Burlington, VT: Vermont Forum on Sprawl, 2003.

New Zealand Ministry for the Environment. *Getting in on the Act: An Everyday Guide to the Resource Management Act of 1991.* Wellington, New Zealand, 2006.

———. *The State of New Zealand's Environment: The State of Our Waters.* Wellington, New Zealand, 2006.

Nivet, Chris. *A Review of Wetland Inventory Information.* Gelderland Province, The Netherlands: Wetlands International, 2002.

North American Waterfowl Management Plan: Continental Progress Assessment, 2005. Washington, DC: U.S. Fish and Wildlife Service, 2005.

Petuch, Edward. *The Geology of the Everglades and Adjacent Areas.* Boca Raton, FL: CRC, 2007.

Ramsar Convention on Wetlands. *Site Summary: Izembek Lagoon National Wildlife Refuge.* Gland, Switzerland: Ramsar Convention, 2003.

———. *Site Summary: Reserva Particular do Patrimonio Natural SESC Pantanal.* Gland, Switzerland: Ramsar Convention, 2003.

———. *Wetlands and the Izembek FishMap Program.* Gland, Switzerland: Ramsar Convention, 2006.

Roll, Gulnara. *Aral Sea: Experience and Lessons Learned.* Washington, DC: World Bank, 2006.

Sever, Megan. "Restoring the River." *Geotimes,* Publication of the American Geological Institute, August 2007.

Shen, Dajun. *Mountain-River-Lake Integrated Water Resources Development Program.* Beijing: China Institute of Water Resources and Hydropower Research, 2006.

Sibbing, Julie. *Nowhere Near No-Net-Loss.* Washington, DC: National Wildlife Federation, 2005.

Status and Trends of Wetlands in the Conterminous United States, 1998 to 2004. Washington, DC: U.S. Fish and Wildlife Service, 2006.

Strand, Margaret. *Wetlands Deskbook.* Washington, DC: Environmental Law Institute, 2001.

Swarts, Frederick. *The Pantanal in the 21st Century.* New York: Hudson MacArthur, 2000.

U.S. Army Corps of Engineers. *National Wetlands Mitigation Action Plan.* Washington, DC: Multiple Agencies (ACOE, NOAA, EPA, FWS, USDA, and FHA), 2002.

U.S. Fish and Wildlife Service. *Izembek National Wildlife Refuge Complex.* Washington, DC: U.S. Department of the Interior, 2004.

———. *Status and Trends of Wetlands in the Conterminous United States.* Washington, DC: U.S. Department of the Interior, 2005.

U.S. Library of Congress. *Wetland Issues.* Washington, DC: Congressional Research Service, 2003.

United Nations. *State of the World Population 2006.* New York: United Nations Population Fund, 2006.

United Nations and the World Meteorological Organization. *Climate Change 2007: The Physical Science Basis.* Geneva, Switzerland: Intergovernmental Panel on Climate Change, 2007.

United Nations Educational, Scientific, and Cultural Organization. *Summary from the International Conference on the Conservation and Sustainable Development of the Danube Delta.* Odessa, Ukraine, 2006.

———. *Water Related Vision for the Aral Sea Basin.* Paris, France: UNESCO, 2000.

United Nations Environment Programme. *Everglades National Park, Florida, USA.* Cambridge, UK: World Conservation Monitoring Centre, 2003.

United Nations Population Fund. *State of the World Population 2006.* New York: United Nations, 2006.

Update on Recent Developments in the Danube Delta. Gland, Switzerland: Ramsar Convention on Wetlands, 2005.

Van Der Valk, Arnold. *The Biology of Freshwater Wetlands.* New York: Oxford University Press, 2006.

Ward, Andy. *Environmental Hydrology.* Boca Raton, FL: Lewis, 2006.

Wetlands International. *Wetlands International: Annual Review, 2005.* Wageningen, The Netherlands: Wetlands International, 2006.

The World Bank. *Little Green Data Book 2007.* Washington, DC: World Bank, 2007.

World Resources Institute. *Millennium Ecosystem Assessment: Wetlands and Water.* Washington, DC: World Resources Institute, 2005.

Index

Italic page numbers indicate images and figures.